AUTISTIC

The ultimate guide to surviving i world

Daniel Millán López

AUTISTIC
The ultimate guide to surviving in the wild neurotypical world

Illustrations by Marisa Martínez Cervantes

English translation by Jai White

© DANIEL MILLÁN LÓPEZ
AUTISTIC: THE ULTIMATE GUIDE TO SURVIVING
IN THE WILD NEUROTYPICAL WORLD

ISBN 978-1-4478-3791-6

English edition

First edition: December 2021
Edited by Lulu.com
All rights reserved.

Except as otherwise provided by law, this book may not be reproduced, neither in whole or in part, nor incorporated into a computer system, or transmitted in any form or by any means (electronic, mechanical, photocopying, recording or otherwise) without the prior written permission of the copyright holders. Infringement of these rights is punishable by law and may constitute a crime against intellectual property.

If you need to photocopy or scan any fragment of this book, contact CEDRO (Centro Español de Derechos Reprográficos)

(www.conlicencia.com; 91 702 19 70 / 93 272 04 47).

To mum

No, I'm not Pablo Iglesias[1].

---

[1] Pablo Iglesias is a Spanish politician famous for his long hair tied back in a ponytail.

Índice

Prologue by Neurodivergente 9

Chapter 1. Introduction 13
Chapter 2. How autism came into my life 21
Chapter 3. What is autism? 27
Chapter 4. Autism diagnosis and labels 33
Chapter 5. Autism and processing 65
Chapter 6. Attention and executive functions 79
Chapter 7. Dichotomous thinking 95
Chapter 8. Mood swings and alexithymia 115
Chapter 9. Empathy and theory of mind 127
Chapter 10. Symbolic understanding 147
Chapter 11. Sensitivity in autism 179
Chapter 12. Social relationships 207
Chapter 13. Anxiety and autism 225
Chapter 14. The masking 259

Epilogue. Sculpting your autistic armour 277

Questionnaires 283

Acknowledgements 303

Sketches 305

Bibliography 311

Prologue by Neurodivergente

The autism spectrum is one of the most-discussed neurodevelopmental conditions in recent years. Despite this, it's perhaps one of the lesser understood in terms of its explanation within medicine. Anyway, I'm not here to talk about that. I'm here to talk about probably the most incredible person and psychology professional I've ever met. You'll know him as Daniel Millán, but for me, he became Dani a long time ago.

But this story wouldn't make sense without the autistic community that welcomed me and de-mystified autism and its expression. I still remember Aida, my best friend, and in many ways, the person who has come to be my saviour, telling me: "You should think about getting a diagnosis. I'm sure you're autistic, and even if I'm wrong, you need support either way". In November 2018, I wrote what was perhaps the hardest email I've ever written. This is the section I found hardest to write, but that which best describes my situation at the time, together with a prescription for methylphenidate and an incorrect diagnosis:

> I really need to know exactly what's going on with me. I feel as though the medication is just isolating me even more than before, as if my sensory issues haven't improved, nor my struggles expressing myself (it's unbelievably difficult for me to verbalise my emotions and thoughts with those who are closest to

me, and I can even smile despite feeling angry or sad). This continues to make socialising with others without everything ending in total disaster, incredibly difficult. People think I'm cold-hearted for slacking in our friendship, or for not understanding boundaries in a conversation. If my diagnosis of ADHD and as being AACC[2] is correct, it would at least help if I knew what type of support and intervention I need, etc.

From that moment onwards, my life changed without me even realising. After just over a month, Dani confirmed my ASC (Autistic Spectrum Condition) diagnosis and we began to work on improving my quality of life, starting by coming off the unnecessary medication. At that time, I was writing my first blog entries based on everything Dani was teaching me. At the end of the sessions, he often told me that he was so excited about writing a book that overhauled the existing information about autism, as well as collating his experiences and knowledge. I asked him "when are you going to start writing your book then?" more than once. That day has finally arrived.

If you're autistic (or think you might be), don't feel bad or think there's something broken inside you. That's how I felt. You're reading the words of not only a specialist, but also those of a friend who wants to bring you closer to your authentic self, free from taboos and fear. Closer to your authentic self, but accompanied by the scientific evidence and Dani's own experience to help. Whether that be because you feel able to use many of the suggested resources yourself, or because you're aware of the less harmful options of still being yourself, but improving your quality of life in whatever way you need. This is a brilliant guide packed with autistic knowledge and

---

[2] AACC refers to a diagnosis of 'Altas Capacidades' in Spain, which is equivalent to being diagnosed as 'Gifted'.

examples given by autistic people, some of whom also form a part of my life.

If you're a professional in this field or someone in your life is autistic, this book is a must for your bookshelf. Although written simply, it doesn't lack objective data, and it gives you a deeper understanding of this unique way of living and being. Not only will it give you a better understanding of autism, it will become that essential handbook to help everyone understand the autistic person in their life.

You'll see that during hard times, this book will prove a great help in terms of supporting the autistic person in your life, and is guaranteed to be respectful, bypassing forceful interventions or actions that try to 'normalise' or 'neurotypicalify' autistic people.

You can dip in and out of the book and flick straight to what you need, or let yourself get totally hooked and not put it down until you've finished. But, most importantly, you'll see that you can come back to the book at any time and it will give at least enough answers to apply them yourself or to guide the autistic person in your life, or perhaps to ask for the right assessment from a specialist, knowing that it will be of use to you.

Dearest Dani, you've achieved the perfect balance between scientific and social realms, between your 'human self' (that I know well), and your 'professional self' (that has helped me so much). Collating our experiences, collecting data and challenging questionable studies is a brave feat, and only someone with such great active listening skills and experience in our community could do it. Thank you for writing this book that I'm sure will revolutionise autism interventions in Spanish-speaking countries. Thank you for your commitment to those of us who sometimes felt as though we didn't have a place in this world. It has been a long time since we discovered that we're not a puzzle that needs putting back together, nor are we all 'blue'. We're perfectly infinite, we need to be listened to, understood and loved unconditionally. You've given me the best gift I could have ever asked for: the ability to embrace my autistic self, and helped me understand and unearth my true identity.

Thank you for being the allistic friend every autistic person needs.

Thank you for your friendship and for letting me write this prologue.

Neurodivergente (@Neurodivergent2)

Chapter 1

Introduction

This might come as a surprise, but I didn't write this book for families of autistic people, although it could provide them with some incredibly valuable information. It's not for my psychology colleagues, either, even though a lot of my explanations can lead to new routes of intervention that they might never have considered. Nor is it for the general public, even though my explanation of autism may influence them to change their dogmatic view and bring them back down to reality. I've written this book predominantly for autistic people. This might throw you off, but I encourage you to keep reading and you'll see why I made this decision.

Not only is it a book aimed predominantly at autistic people; it's written using inclusive language. I know that at first it might sound strange in your head: that happened to me, too. Even some autistic people (with their engrained sense of specificity and perfectionism) find it hard to accept the use of inclusive language. But believe me, your mind will automatically become accustomed to these changes, and it really doesn't take much effort.

Inclusive language is a communicative proposal that aims to deconstruct gender conventions in terms of language. It aims to separate gender from biological sex, and include women, men, non-binary people or those who live beyond traditional conventions, in everyday language. The use of this language is defended by some and challenged by others. To start with, the Royal Spanish Academy (RAE) demonstrates its zealous disapproval of its use[3]. Yes, the same academy that say it reflects current language use by incorporating words such as *wasap* (in reference to the instant messaging application WhatsApp), or *almóndiga* (a vulgarism of the word *albondiga*, or 'meatball' in English). This same institution states: "In our language (Spanish), the male grammatical distinction works, as in others, as an inclusive term to refer to mixed groups, or in generic or non-specific contexts" (2019). As in psychiatry (we'll see in various parts of this book), institutions that oversee and judge the diagnosis or speech rules that are often a far cry from social evolution: "The use of inclusive language advances expeditiously among young people and social media is witness to this movement, but where does it fit into more formal contexts in which – it would appear – they are more resistant? It is not unusual to think that in these spaces, the most common rules are followed" (López, 2018).

The majority of the autistic community has opted for inclusive language, and the rest consider its use to be valid, despite not using it frequently. This community shares a history of not only discrimination, but also direct negation of its mere existence, as is the case for other communities, such as the trans community (in issues that vary from social recognition of binary trans people to non-binary people). If, at the end of the day, the goal goes beyond that of inclusion and equality, what better reason to use a type of language that makes everyone

---

[3] As expressed in the *Libro de estilo de la lengua española según la norma panhispánica* (2018).

feel represented? As stated by Giacchetta (2018): "I can imagine how immensely healing it is for a diverse identity such as my own, or even for other many realities – such as intersex people - to find themselves in a place where they are welcomed, allowed to express their gender with no conditions nor standards that were not created for everyone. Also, how liberating it must be to not have to explain their mere existence, because at the end of the day, we all want the same thing: to exist". She adds: "The use of the letter 'e'[4] enables a clear reference to gender diversity, contributing to the overthrowing of linguistic asymmetries in order to build a fairer and less violent society".

The same goes for the terminology used to refer to autism: should we call it Autism Spectrum Disorder (ASD) or Autism Spectrum Condition (ASC)? Should we say 'person with autism' or 'autistic person'? Which is correct? Generally speaking, those who tend to support the use of person 'with autism' and autism spectrum 'disorder' are families of autistic people, or professionals. Those who use these terms to refer to the autistic community tend to believe that a diagnosis is a 'label' that removes the person and only recognises their autism, only defining them based on the disorder or their associated difficulties. Those who refer to themselves as 'autistic people' embrace their condition as something that defines them, not something that restricts them, nor an illness they want to get rid of, of course. Some people with autistic relatives (especially children) tend to accuse the autistic community of romanticising autism as though their mild autism or Asperger's were a sort of 'five-star autism', free of challenges in comparison to their more severely affected relatives. In part, this book aims to

---

[4] The letter "e" is used in the Spanish language in order to express gender neutrality. It is the equivalent to using the singular 'they' in English.

demonstrate that the nucleus of autistic processing remains the same, regardless of the impact of these difficulties and the potential differences that can be identified when it comes to the daily challenges faced by someone on one end of the spectrum and someone on the other.

I prefer to say 'autistic person' or 'person on the spectrum'. I'll explain why throughout the book. Of course, I'll always respect the choice made by each individual regarding how they refer to themselves or their loved one, but I think that reflecting on the choice of one term or another is more important than it first appears (beyond the linguistic debate), because it demonstrates the epistemological[5] point of departure of each person in terms of what autism is.

On the other hand, you'll also see that I alternate between expressions such as 'People on the spectrum tend to…' or, on the other hand, 'As people on the spectrum, you tend to…'. I find that referring to 'you' or 'you all' over and over again can sound too much like an order, so I've alternated between them according to the specific circumstances of the narrative. This will also enable non-autistic people to relate to what I'm describing. That's part of the aim of this book: to bridge those necessary gaps to provoke significant change in interaction, which requires both sides need to make an effort. After all, this is the greatest challenge faced by people on the spectrum: interacting with their surroundings.

As I mentioned at the start of this introduction, this is a book written predominantly for autistic people. No less intriguing is the lack of autistic voices in the professional practice of scien-

---

[5] Epistemology is the aspect of philosophy that studies principles, foundations, extension and methods of human knowledge.

tific dissemination that only takes them into account as a semi-statistic to test theories and data, utterly dehumanising the people it discusses. With the exception of autistic authors, it's rare to find a book about autism in which the authors speak directly to people on the spectrum. It's time for anyone who works in the field of autism to start doing it.

I'm not trying to write an informative book as such, or at least not in the more 'academic' sense of the word. Although, I want anyone who gets hold of this book to understand the true nature of the autism spectrum from an up-to-date perspective (and that of almost two decades of work in this field). That's why I prefer to look at it as an exercise of truly understanding those aspects I deem most important when it comes to explaining the complex condition that is autism. This also includes families, as well as all the professionals who work with autistic people, whether children or adults. This is a guide in which I explain the processes that underlie autism, to be able to locate these in the social context of people on the spectrum, and to provide a series of tools to enable both autistic people and the people in their lives to find the right path towards better and fairer interactions. As I'll go on to explain in the different chapters, there's nothing wrong about being autistic: what is truly unfair is the cruel demand of our surroundings on autistic people (and the unrealistic societal expectations).

The information in this book is organised inthemed chapters. To give a complete psychological explanation for a condition as diverse as autism is to embark on an incredibly challenging, if not impossible task. The best way I've come across to explain each of the different processes in autism is to separate them, but always being aware that no one process can be explained without another. This way, once you've read the entire book, you'll be able to go back to the specific information you need at any given time. After the introductions (prologue, this introduction and the following chapter, in which I explain why I chose to specialise in autism), each chapter explores a key topic in terms of understanding the idiosyncrasies of autism, and I include a series of tips in the form of a guide for each of these processes (chapters 4 to 11). I then draw together everything I've explained regarding its impact on social relationships (chapter 12), to then end with some of the consequences of this defective interaction with our surroundings (chapters 13 and 14). I end with an epilogue complete with some tips, as a sort of "quick guide", followed by a series of autism detection screening tests[6] and a questionnaire about masking[7] in autistic adults.

In this book you'll come across many references to studies and professional opinions, but I really wanted to highlight the importance of the testimony of the true protagonists: autistic people. You'll also come across lots of footnotes (which you've probably already noticed). As well as the common references to authors, studies, technical terms, quotes, etc., I explain each instance of non-literal language I use throughout the book. This is another reason why I've chosen to use a more laid-back style of writing, far from the pedantic professional or academic style, so as to make it as accessible as possible.

The incredible front cover designed by Marisa Martínez will have grabbed your attention right away. Marisa is an outstanding autistic artist and I've been lucky enough to be able to work with her on this project. Communication with her has

---

[6] Screening tests are quick tests used to determine a potential disorder, disease or condition.

[7] Masking is a behaviour used by some people on the spectrum. See chapter 14.

been phenomenal right from the start, and I couldn't be happier with her work, as she has transformed each of the situations I described to her, exceptionally and admirably – autistic style! As you'll see, many of the illustrations she's created for this book describe situations experienced by people on the spectrum with a sense of humour. We decided to do it this way so as to combine, on the one hand, overwhelming respect for the community and on the other, to demystify the notion that autistic people don't have a sense of humour. It's common for autistic people to use memes[8] to describe situations linked to their literal understanding and also to highlight the lack of understanding of their condition within society. If you're on the spectrum, you'll probably relate to lots of the situations we describe. In fact, Marisa has chosen to include herself in some of them. Similarly, lots of the captions under the illustrations and diagrams include ironic or sarcastic comments. Many of the situations that surround the world of autism are so absurd and unfair that humour transforms it into a cathartic exercise.

Lots of people have asked me why it has taken me so long to publish this book. I've responded endless times: I really get stuck in[9]. I've always seen myself as more of a war correspondent than a TV presenter. I've always considered academic work to be secondary throughout my professional career. There has always been something more urgent to tend to: a child having a rough time, a teen who couldn't understand why they were unable to make friends, or an adult experiencing suicidal thoughts. I should also acknowledge that I haven't always felt at ease within the professional environment, which

---

[8] A meme is a concept, idea, situation or feeling that is expressed virtually, such as through images.
9 A non-literal expression that refers to getting involved, working closely with people on their level.

notably talks about people on the spectrum, systematically denying them a voice, speaking of the grief families go through, as if autistic people were just beings, or worse, things. Even today we come across situations like these, but fortunately signs of change are on the horizon.

I've been involved in several projects throughout my life: from managing one of Spain's largest autism centres to participating in ground-breaking work placement programmes. I've mourned the disregard for both effort and talent at the hands of dreadful management. I haven't always made the right decisions on my professional journey, but I can assure you that my overall aim has been to be more useful to autistic people.

I'm now clear that bridging the gap between the autistic community and the rest of the world is one of my top priorities. We can only change the paradigm and view as to what autism actually is by creating an understanding of the autistic condition. The time has come for the non-autistic members of society to make most of the effort. After all, it has been 78 years of neurotypical injustice.

Chapter 2

How autism came into my life

"Daniel, you're ignorant" (Juanjo, 14, talking to me).

When I was finishing my psychology degree in about 2000, I was also working alongside my studies or looking after young people with a variety of conditions. The majority had diverse social difficulties. I've always got along well with children and teenagers, and making a connection and relationships built on trust have come easily. This is mostly because of my appearance, but also my hobbies, which usually fit in nicely with those of younger people. During my youth, it wasn't cool to be a comic fan. In fact, it made you anything but: if you were still reading The Avengers[10] comics after a certain age, you were more than likely to be made fun of by your classmates.

When working with young people, really connecting with their interests and hobbies is key. When I see the offices of some of the other professionals out there, it's not at all surprising that some kids are simply terrified. With bookshelves reminiscent of a law firm and professionals draped in white coats, I wonder how they can create an environment of trust that allows for a

---

[10] *The Avengers* is a North American comic published by Marvel Comics.

good therapeutic relationship. That should be the goal for the first few sessions; finding that link based on hobbies, interests and preferences. Young people are often 'forced' to attend appointments, so we should at least make this a time during which they can feel valued in those areas where they're normally neglected by adults.

A teenager's bookshelf? No, that's just my office.

I started to work with one of these young people. His parents wanted him to get involved in lots of sports to burn off some of his energy. They told me he was very 'intense'. He was 12 years old and adopted, just like his sister. His adoptive father was a psychiatrist and psychoanalyst. His parents knew I'd always been into sports and asked me to take him out on a walk. They warned me about his obsessive thoughts. I'm sure you can already tell where this is going, and it will become even clearer, but at the time, nobody knew what was wrong, not even his father. I can't be sure of this, but he was probably incredibly frustrated, especially given his job.

They were right, he was intense. Incredibly so. He was absolutely obsessed with Pokémon. He knew each and every Pokémon going, its attacks, type and he acted them out. He could spend two hours explaining everything and he was incredibly excited about it, showing you each and every movement, one by one. When he began telling you about something, he did a strange ritual: he'd hit a table, railing, or whatever was in reach, with both hands, and then hit himself on the forehead. He actually really hurt himself at times.

Sometimes he threw impressive tantrums. Once he grabbed a kitchen knife and followed his family around the house. They were forced to hide. He also had a very bizarre way of walking. He appeared to have a significant lack of coordination when it came to moving his body. Interestingly, he was great at drawing. He always drew the same thing, but he did it well.

Anyway, on one of our outings, we were chatting about zoology, a topic he was very interested in and his knowledge was unusual for his age. At one point we were talking about kangaroos, I couldn't remember the name of the marsupial this species belongs to and my mind went blank. I said "Those animals that have the pouch thing, ummm…" and he blurted "Marsupials, ignorant" at me.

He said that to me and carried on talking as if nothing had happened. I mean, if someone says something like that, with such fervour, the other person would feel angry or await a response. Nothing. I was shocked, but at the same time, it was incredibly revealing. For me it was fundamental to check that this person hadn't insulted me, but he didn't understand why, more often than not, this could be considered an insult (as you can imagine, he didn't have any friends at all).

I started to do some research. My degree touched on autism, but only very briefly. I came across Asperger's. Everything fit, even things that weren't included in the DSM I'd been pouring over[11]. He had overwhelming auditory sensitivity, as well as a sensitive scalp. He had several rituals he had to carry out so as not to end up having a meltdown. He never seemed to remember me, or my name[12]. His language was incredibly advanced for his age, but his use of pragmatics was somewhat less unusual, and there were prosodic alterations[13]... Everything made sense. The possible hypotheses given previously (and more so with those supposed 'attacks' he suffered), were going to have a significant impact on his life and were simply, wrong. Fortunately, he was diagnosed with Asperger's and attended a special education centre for children on the spectrum.

I continued working with him for a while. I remember I taught him a different ritual to do before telling his stories (clap his hands hard a few times before starting), to stop him from hurting his head, and a few other things. Lots of other things happened and I've got plenty of anecdotes from my time with him, some of which still help me to explain some processes typical of autism. The thing is, from the day he called me igno-

---

[11] In this context, it is used in a non-literal sense to express "research" or "deep reading".

[12] *Prosopagnosia*, see chapter 11.

[13] The pragmatics of language refers to the way it is adapted to different contexts.

rant onwards, I've dedicated my professional career to autism. I'm very happy with that decision.

I honestly think that to work in the field of neurodivergence you need to have been through experiences like this one, ones that make you brush off[14] your prejudgment (based on your values and the way you perceive reality) and understand that there are different ways of understanding the world and, therefore, of expressing yourself, all of which are equality as valid, or perhaps even more valid than your own.

---

[14] Used in a non-literal sense to express "forgetting" or "overlooking".

Chapter 3

What is autism?

"For me, my autism has been the instruction manual my parents lost when I was born. This has helped me to understand, discover and love myself and my children" (Carolina, 36 years old).

When someone is looking for information about autism, at a time where knowledge is easy to access, it's still unbelievable that the majority of the information you come across, especially on social media, is not only just wrong, but often totally surreal. Today, there's no real way of controlling the information posted online, and anyone can start a blog and write whatever they want. It's then down to the reader to decide how much of the information they believe.

Although it might seem harmless, it can be devastating for someone looking for information about symptoms they've observed in themselves or a loved one. In this day and age, it's our first port of call[15], isn't it? If we've got a question, we just Google it. The issue is, what pops up isn't based on how accu-

---

[15] Used in a non-literal sense to express "the first place we look" for something.

rate the information is, but many other variables, such as how many visits that webpage has received, the advertisement budget that page has been able to invest in search engines, your search history, and many more.

This means you'll find diverse versions of the initial impressions of autism: from being a contagious disease, to a disorder caused by telephone aerials located on the roofs of buildings in major cities. Not even to mention the most absurd theories made up by religious fanatics, these interpretations of autism tend to agree that autism is a disease, or at least a disorder, and is caused by an external factor or entity.

Fortunately, the majority of us come across more accurate information about autism, and despite some scientific publications being in dire need of an update, the first impression is somewhat closer to the truth, or at least to that which prevails in the realms of medicine, psychiatry and psychology. But even in these cases we need to be careful of where we get our information from.

For example, even from this scientific perspective, some psychoanalytical models continue to be ingrained in their archaic and completely vilified vision of autism as childhood psychosis. What they don't tend to mention is that in reality, this was not the case, in part because there was no other way of doing it. They had a choice of situating themselves within this paradigm, or not being able to present their studies. Something similar happened to Grunya Sukhareva (1925) two decades prior. Although her studies are lesser known, despite having described autism as its own entity prior to her peers, they also positioned it in the only possible place: as part of a schizophrenic psychopathy. This doesn't mean to say that part of the conceptualisation of autism according to these three authors was not one of firm belief of autism as a type of psychosis. However, even though Asperger abandoned this model later on, Kanner continued to maintain it and made several public declarations that continue to do significant harm, even to date.

From a clinical perspective, autism has been viewed as a completely different entity to schizoid disorders for decades. However, in contrary to all the assessment and diagnostic manuals, some schools of analytical thought continue to uses these offensive paradigms, perpetuating harm, both to autistic people and their families, with theories such as that of 'refrigerator mothers'[16] and other pseudoscientific ideas with nothing to fall back on, such as autism being caused by sexual trauma (Pelegrin, 1991). According to some of these professionals, as regards the treatment of autism, "[…] we find ourselves faced with fundamental interrogations: the process of constitutions of the subject and its coordinates; femininity and maternal function articulated around the phallus; psychosis in childhood; transference in psychosis; and, moreover, in infantile psychoses" (Jerusalinsky, 1997).

Luckily there are increasingly less people who use these terms when talking about autism and there's a current scientific consensus that autism is linked to neurobiological development and has a significant genetic component. A person is born autistic, and their relationship with their parents has nothing to do with it. Likewise, the myth that vaccines cause autism is backed predominantly by evidence that proves it to be false. In fact, according to the Spanish Autism Federation (2020), this

---

[16] In 1948, in *Time* magazine, Leo Kanner blamed the families of his patients for having cause their children's autism as a result of a lack of love and adequate care. Specifically, he blamed the mother for having emotionally neglected her children in order to prioritise her own professional career.

myth "[…] is a result of studies that have been proven to be both fraudulent and backed by financial interests". They take advantage that the age at which certain vaccines are administered, at around 18 months old, tends to coincide with the appearance of some autism symptoms, to assure they are the cause. But as we know, correlation does not mean causality.

On the other hand, and to name just one of the many other myths about autism, the belief that autism was intrinsically linked to males (something that I've always thought was absurd), is increasingly being proven to be false; insofar as diagnostic models are evolving and tools designed to detect autism in women are being designed. This evolution in terms of its detection will continue to improve if, once and for all, we stop searching for autism triggers in our surroundings and focus resources on updating our perspective of autism, including its specific presentation in women.

The world of autism is surrounded by opportunistic individuals. The impact of this condition on parents tends to be so significant that they dedicate their lives to doing whatever they can for their children, which is totally understandable. What can they do if the professional who diagnoses their child tells them they have an irreversible illness? Well, go in search of a cure. And as science has nothing to offer them, they look for the miraculous cure anywhere possible. Also, if they tell the parents to weigh up years of therapy on the one hand, and rumours, spells or diluted bleach on the other, it's understandable (not acceptable) that they go for the quickest and easiest option.

For decades, instead of trying to understand autism, even in terms of approaches that are supposedly scientific and ethical, people on the spectrum have been made invisible. The famous method developed by Ivar Lovaas in the 80s, Applied Behavioural Analysis (ABA) had exactly that goal in mind: transform the identity of the autistic person. There are many traumatic stories recalled by people on the spectrum who remember these interventions as being genuine abuse. Among other things, the idea was to stop them from stimming, whereas today, we now know that these are mechanisms of emotional self-regulation, in some ways similar to nervous leg shaking or chewing on a pen lid for a neurotypical person.

As autistic author Christine Lion (2020) said:

> Curing autism is not impossible, and if it were, it would transform you into a completely different person. Autism is not a 'layer' added onto a neurotypical person, but a complete series of skills and challenges that make you unique.

While the archetype of autism as an illness, or in its more diluted form, disorder, still stands, some people will look for the easy option: this could be anything from pseudo therapy to medication or therapy where my child spends an hour a week in a room and miraculously improves without us even having to do anything.

Only by way of the conception of autism as a form of neurodivergence and a different way of perceiving the world, will we be able to help change how it is seen and understood. This conceptual transformation will come as a result of changing the world, not autistic people.

It's still surprising that the vision of autism, its mere definition, remains conditioned by the view of a clinical professional, insofar as it is still framed from the perspective of a disorder. Although I openly challenge this classification, as you'll see throughout this book, in that case, it would seem that people who are diagnosed with a disorder are treated as if they were no longer human beings with their own desires, free will and voice. A diagnosis does define you: you're autistic, but that doesn't mean you're no longer a person.

Until very recently, autistic people were never given credit, and what they had to say about autism was all but ignored. But, doesn't the fact that they want to express what autism means to them make perfect sense?

Chapter 4

Autism diagnosis and labels

"I have dreadful memories of my assessment. It was all done on the same day, and I spent hours and hours doing tests. I then had to wait a month for them to call me and give me my diagnosis. I didn't have autism. How could I be autistic if I looked people in the eye and had a job?" (Marian, 42 years old)

Diagnosis. Broadly speaking, we could perhaps define it as a necessary action undertaken when someone feels as though something isn't quite right. Diagnosis is a process that identifies the ultimate cause of this unease. More specifically, the diagnostic process consists of collating information to later analyse and interpret it, allowing us to assess a certain condition.

When it comes to autism, we're talking about a type of neurodivergence that has absolute potential to go unnoticed. Late diagnoses outweigh early diagnoses. According to the World Health Organisation (WHO), 1 in every 165 people is autistic (2021). This number varies between countries. For example, it is much greater in the United States: 1 in every 54 people is autistic (Autism and Developmental Disabilities Monitoring Network, 2021). The fact that there are differences between countries depends greatly on the effectiveness of early diagnosis measures. And although there is little data from less developed countries, autism as global phenomenon has been more than proven. It is present in all types of populations, regardless of race, gender or culture.

So, do these early detection methods work? Despite having improved, their effectiveness depends on a number of factors. In many cases, the 'severity' of the symptoms can have a fundamental impact. People on the spectrum who have more significant difficulties; children who don't start talking when expected of them if they were to develop normatively, who have behavioural disorders or a comorbid condition, such as epilepsy disorders, are easier to detect. On the contrary, profiles more similar to those recognised as Asperger's syndrome are diagnosed very late, often later than 6 years of age. Other people don't receive their diagnosis until adulthood, having spent half their life feeling, at the very least, like a strange species in society. In many cases, especially when it comes to women, their diagnosis was ruled out as young girls, and they later go on to receive an autism diagnosis in adulthood.

Wrong planet, perhaps?

Because of how diagnostic protocols are designed today, professionals have to follow official assessment manuals with international recognition. The most widely accepted classification system is the DSM (Diagnostic and Statistical Manual of Mental Disorders), the diagnostic and statistical manual by the American Psychiatric Association. This manual contains descriptions, symptoms and criteria to diagnose.... Mental disorders. That's right, even today autism continues to be considered a mental disorder in the realms of psychiatry (among others).

So, what's a mental disorder? Is it a synonym for disease, like many people think it is? According to the latest edition of the DSM (5th, 2013): "A mental disorder is a syndrome characterized by clinically significant disturbance in an individual's cognition, emotion regulation, or behaviour that reflects a dysfunction in the psychological, biological, or development processes underlying mental functioning". Well, here we're talking about 'dysfunction', not disease, in any case. Dysfunction is defined as an alteration in terms of undertaking an action in a specific context.

According to the WHO (2006):

> A mental or behavioural disorder is characterised by a disturbance in intellectual activity, mood or behaviour that is not in keeping with cultural norms and beliefs. In most cases, symptoms are accompanied by distress and interference in personal functions.

Ah, "Disturbance […] that is not in keeping with cultural norms and beliefs". And, as we all know, norms and beliefs cannot be changed over time, right? I'm being sarcastic. What I'm trying to say is that many of the definitions of what is 'normal' or not, or 'non-normative' or not, depend greatly on the time at which that divergence occurs.

Clinical criteria manuals are by no means absolute truth. In fact, they undergo continuous review processes. From the first edition of the DSM in 1952 to the most recent edition published in 2013, numerous reviews, changes and new terms have been added. This process has by no means been free of controversy, and what has become clear is that, unfortunately, the APA is always one step behind the social and human progress being made. To give just one example, everyone had to wait for the second edition of the manual, published in 1973, to remove homosexuality from the sexual deviance section included in the DSM.

Will the same thing happen with autism? Will it be removed from the DSM as a type of mental disorder? Personally, I hope so. But just like with homosexuality, we can't expect that this change to come from such a closed-minded institution as the APA. This organisation will need to be pressured by the autistic community and the professionals who actually work with people on the spectrum from an integrational perspective, not in a condescending, paternalistic and clinical manner. It understands autism not just as a disorder, but as a disease with no cure. I'm not saying this is always the case, but when I come across professionals with this point of view, I genuinely believe that they haven't seen an autistic person outside of their offices or clinics.

For Carolina, mother of two children on the spectrum and herself diagnosed autistic, replacing disorder with condition is fundamental: "For me, this means that it will go from being seen as a disease to a condition that forms part of who we are, and isn't something to avoid or get rid of".

However, for Cristina, an autistic teacher, this change is necessary, but it still has consequences: "For me it would mean that our fight to prevent our way of perceiving reality being pathologised would take an enormous step forward, both officially and in terms of bureaucracy. I'm afraid that this could cause us to lose support, because they think we can just 'get through it, regardless', but I think it's an essential step towards normalising and making our neurotype visible".

Actions from within the majority of the autistic community have shown overwhelming support for this change.

Autistic pride.

Going back to diagnosis, as I mentioned, as professionals we're obliged to use this reference manual or similar, such as those by the WHO or ICD (International Classification of Diseases), which is currently on its 11th edition. For me, the clinical criteria based on symptoms are not enough to undertake an autism assessment and, on the other hand, it isn't fair to do it this way if you genuinely understand autism as a type of neurodivergence.

In medicine, a differential diagnosis is the procedure undertaken to identify a specific disease by ruling out other potential causes that have a clinical profile similar to that with which the patient presents. In our case, undertaking a diagnosis following this process is essential, as many of the symptoms associated with autism, and are commonly known, are not exclusive to autism.

Shall we put it to the test? We'll start by using a series of popular concepts about the nature of autism before moving on to more technical ones.

Is stimming exclusive to autism? No, no it's not.
Recurring interests? No.
The (supposed) lack of interest in peers? No.

Let's go one step further[17]:
Executive dysfunction? Actually, no.
Dichotomous thinking? No, not at all.
Hypersensitivity? No.

What I'm trying to get at is that if we start to notice certain things (these symptoms, for example) and we look on the internet, it's highly likely they will lead us to autism. Potentially, in addition to articles we might come across, we'll read some autistic people's experiences, alongside others. Careful. Experiences are very personal and a lot of what is described are symptoms. If we want to get to the root cause, we need to identify their origin and, with some difficulty, we could do a Google search. When undertaking a differential diagnosis, the main criteria to ascertain whether or not a symptom is related to autism is to identify its nature.

---

[17] Non-literal expression. In this context it refers to using more complex terminology.

Sometimes people say to me: "I'm not interested in a diagnosis, what I'm looking for are tools to help me address certain situations". Personally, I never start working without at least a minimal prior analysis, and in an ideal situation we would have an accurate differential diagnosis. Otherwise, the intervention strategies may not only be ineffective, but counterproductive. Diagnosis is fundamental to the definition of the nature of the difficulties faced. Once established, we can then choose the appropriate tool.

There are a series of conditions that although very different to autism, can present very similar symptoms. I'm sure we can all think of at least a few, right? For children with language issues, there are speech disorder diagnoses. If it appears there might be issues with attention, ADHD/ADD (Attention Deficit and/or Hyperactivity Disorder) is on the cards[18]. With obsessions, obsessive compulsive disorder (OCD) may be mentioned. And if we're talking about a case in which there have been instances of hospitalisation or even admissions, we could consider Borderline Personality Disorder or schizophrenia… But that's not it. This is exactly why an assessment should be very systematic, to rule out a potential origin (nature) of the symptoms other than autism, before "jumping" to undertake an autism assessment.

The process should be the same when it's the other way around: many autistic people have received a variety of incorrect diagnoses that may have led them to question their very existence (and even commit suicide). Instances of autistic women with (incorrect) Borderline Personality Disorder diagnoses are becoming increasingly common. An ED (Eating

---

[18] A non-literal expression that means something is considered or is a possibility or option.

Disorder) is one of the disorders that masks the most diagnoses of autism in women (Gillberg, 1983, and more recently, Baron-Cohen, 2013), and not to mention anxiety and depression...

Which areas must be assessed in autism? In my opinion, there are three main areas to be assessed, where the divergence of autism reveals a difference in processing when compared to the neurotypical perception (in addition to other conditions or disorders):

- The symbolic area.
- The mentalist skills area.
- The information processing area.

Some colleagues or people with theoretical knowledge of autism could argue that these areas have nothing to do with Wing's triad[19]. Yes and no. In my experience, if significant care is not taken, many of the aspects assessed by Wing's triad can just stay on the surface. Communication and social interaction factors can be based on a deficit in theory of mind (anticipation of the thoughts and intentions of others), in addition to a specific processing type (sequential). Cognitive inflexibility is not exclusive to autism (ADHD, manic-depressive disorder, OCD....) and therefore, we need to explore its nature.

Having broken down these areas, the aspects to be assessed should be (at least) the following:

1. Socio-emotional comprehension.
2. Communication and language.

---

[19] Lorna Wing (1928-2014) was one of the main contributors to the study of autism from an integrational perspective and that of knowledge of the condition.

3. Neuropsychological functions.
4. Cognitive abilities.
5. Emotional assessment.

At the end of this process, and once an autism diagnosis has been established (on the condition that the pertinent clinical criteria are met), we must specify. Yes, dear colleagues, you've got to get stuck into it[20]. In certain cases, especially in (very) young children, it can be difficult to reach a clear conclusion or the assessment pathway may not have allowed for a differential diagnosis and, therefore, the 'developmental delay' label is used, which in itself is not a diagnosis. This name simply means that something is going on, we don't know why, and we don't know how it's going to evolve.

If this is not the case, we need to specify. When the fourth edition of the DSM was valid (until May 2013), autism fell into the General Developmental Delay (GDD) classification. The name alone couldn't have been worse: it doesn't indicate a disorder in all areas of the person's development, but in "certain developmental areas". This is what is known in autism as "evolutionary disharmony": the manual describes some developmental areas as being significantly affected and others appear to be unaffected. In which case, the GDD could be one of the following:

- Autism Spectrum Disorder.
- Asperger's Syndrome.
- Rett Syndrome.
- Childhood Disintegrative Disorder.
- Global Developmental Delay.

---

[20] In this context, this non-literal expression means to be specific and offer a deeper explanation.

The latter was used as a sort of hotchpotch diagnosis[21]. It was used when there was no question about someone having some form of global developmental delay (GDD), but they didn't quite fit the criteria for any of the other options, and this diagnostic criterion was generally used as a form of elimination. Anyway, before going on to explain these 'disorders', I want to make it clear that GDD as a final diagnosis is incomplete, or better said, wrong. I wanted to mention that as throughout my career I've come across lots of reports that have given this diagnosis.

Autism spectrum disorder defined the 'nuclear' autism disorder established by Leo Kanner (1943). This diagnosis was given to those people who were considered to be the most severely affected. They didn't have any spoken language, with either none or little intention to communicate (we'd have to look into why, but that's a different story), incredibly inflexible and with very limited symbolic abilities. This diagnosis was often accompanied by several comorbidities, such as epilepsy-type disorders. Due to the differences in terms of the samples chosen to analyse the prevalence of this comorbidity, the percentage varies significantly, but today it is said to be between 20% and 65%, compared to 2% within the neurotypical population.

We then have Asperger's syndrome (called a syndrome by the ICD. Which sounds worse? disorder or syndrome?). Despite publishing his studies at the same time as Kanner, they weren't taken into consideration until the 80s, (partly thanks to the work undertaken by Lorna Wing, who brought it back from the side-lines). Here it describes verbal people, with different, 'less severe' difficulties, more centred on social interaction and

---

[21] A colloquial expression used to refer to a series of different, disorganised things.

limited interests. Interestingly, one of the exclusion criteria for Asperger's was that there could not be any delay in language acquisition. This criterion was heavily criticised by many autism professionals (among whom I include myself) and, in fact, some of us 'daredevils' didn't take it into account when diagnosing Asperger's.

Rett syndrome is a very severe disorder that affects many developmental areas, and generally speaking, has a very limited prognosis. It predominantly affects the female population, although some cases have been identified in the male population. I remember diagnosing someone many years ago, when I led the Badajoz Centre for Autism.

Childhood Disintegrative Disorder was a rare disorder. It tends to be characterised by normative development in terms of acquisition of abilities, followed by their sudden loss. This is similar to the 'regression' that is observed in some Kanner-type cases of autism, but in these cases the loss is more abrupt. It has sometimes been named Heller syndrome (1908) or disintegrative psychosis. This name will give you an idea as to what sort of paradigm occurred. It has always been one of the most controversial categories within GDDs and, it is currently classified outside of the types of autism, as is the case with Rett syndrome. I've only seen two children with this diagnosis throughout my career.

So, where does the term ASD fit in? because it's nowhere to be seen in the DSM-IV. In fact, GDD is mentioned as opposed to ASD. But before the DSM5 (we'll get there), the term Autism Spectrum Disorder was already being used, as we owe it to Lorna Wing, who we've already mentioned, and who together with Judith Gould (1979), defined the 'autistic continuum' (or spectrum). Perhaps *contínuo* would have been a better translation into Spanish, as spectrum has never really meant anything to me.

Thanks, DSM5.

According to these authors, "autism is just a series of symptoms that can be associated with different neurobiological disorders and very varied intellectual levels". In other words: All people with GDD had ASD, but not all people with ASD had GDD. This image demonstrates it well:

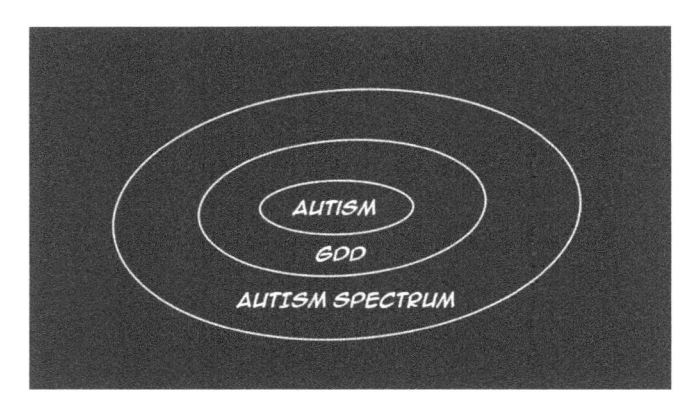

Autism, GDD and ASD.

According to this image, there are 'primary' and 'secondary' autisms. So, people who are born autistic, because the root of their nature (and, from a clinical perspective, their difficulties) are defined by autism. However, there is also another group of people who are considered 'secondary', as the autism is not the origin, but depending on their development they 'acquire' symptoms or needs compatible with autism; or some more profound characteristics, even perceptive, which make them similar to autism. In this second group we are talking about generic conditions or disorders such as Fragile X, tuberous sclerosis, Wiedemann-Steiner syndrome… But there are also other people with types of hearing or visual difficulties. Are these people autistic? No. GDD? No. But they could have ASD.

Ultimately, the conclusion, according to the creators of the term ASD, is that as regards the diagnostic label, the symptomatologic alterations of the spectrum (as a result of the interaction of neurodivergence with the surroundings) and the location of the different dimensions are what define treatment strategies and not the labels that define the profiles.

Things were already complicated, but the arrival of the DSM5 came with another blow[22]. I think the inclusion of the term ASD was necessary, but they've changed its meaning so much so that it has entirely lost its original meaning and has led to significant confusion.

In the DSM5 (which has been used since 18th May 2013), Rett syndrome is a separate diagnosis from the autistic condition (although it can be referred to as an association condition), as in the case with pervasive developmental disorder. On the other hand, Asperger's syndrome and General Developmental Delay have been. removed. Now there is only one diagnostic criteria: ASD. However, some specifics need to be highlighted, such as whether or not there is an accompanying intellectual impairment, an accompanying language impairment, whether it is associated with a medical or genetic condition (partially respecting the origins of the term ASD here), or whether it is associated with another neurodevelopmental, mental or behavioural disorder. It also establishes three levels of support requirements.

- Level 1: requires support.
- Level 2: requires substantial support.
- Level 3: requires very substantial support.

The description of the different support levels is so poor that they are insufficient even in an undeniable case of autism, and the assigning of each support level is at the discretion and perception of the needs of the person whom the professional is

---

[22] Used in a colloquial sense meaning to worsen what had already occurred.

assessing. Also, only two incredibly broad areas are observed: social communication and restricted and repetitive behaviours.

By making such a radical change to the classification model, many people who had previously been diagnosed ended up wondering Now what? It would appear logical that level 1 would correspond to Asperger's syndrome and level 3 to Kanner's autism, with level 2 as more of a 'midpoint'. Well, it's not that simple. If we take into consideration the support requirements, we can frame an Asperger's-type profile that could fit perfectly into level 2. And, in certain circumstances, even level 3! So, currently, diagnosis depends on your support needs. It isn't set in stone[23].

On the other hand, if the intention was, as has been mentioned in different places, to put an end to this perception of Asperger's syndrome as a type of "5-star autism"[24], and generate better cohesion of the world of autism and its community, the result is an absolute fiasco. This is exactly what has been happening with the level system: demonising level 3 autism as being severe and beyond saving and minimising the impact of a diagnosis of level 1 autism. On many occasions, I've had families contact me with concerns about the concept of these levels. They've even told me that when they've received the diagnosis, is just says "ASD", without going into more detail. If the DSM5 had already made it hard, we're making it even more complicated.

---

[23] Used in a non-literal sense to express something that is not fixed. It can be changeable.
[24] Based on the idea that people with Asperger's-type profiles did not face any challenges when compared with Kanner-type autism profiles.

At the end of the day, the levels or support levels are not used to identify a person as having an Asperger or Kanner profile, for example. Nor are they used to establish whether or not it's a case of high or low functioning autism (eugh). Its function is to get an idea of support needs, based on a complete profile with much more information. This profile should be created with significant information from the different areas in which they may have difficulties or deficits, to use clinical lingo. I prefer to highlight the areas in which conflict occurs as regards divergence in interactions with their surroundings.

Each of these areas (we'll use the symbolic area, which for me is a fundamental part of understanding autism and which we'll see in chapter 10 onwards) includes a collection of information that we must know in order to give the person appropriate tools, as opposed to general tools, for many reasons:

1) If we use a tool that doesn't take into consideration the idiosyncrasies of autism, it's likely that not only will it be unsuccessful, it will be a disaster. This is one of the reasons why "conventional" therapy doesn't work with autistic people, and the diagnostic label has a very clear function here: if you're looking for support, it should be specialist support.
2) If we use a strategy that's above the person's 'level', especially when it comes to children, this can end in disaster. Autistic people tend to have a very low frustration tolerance, and using a tool that exceeds their abilities can lead the person on the spectrum to sink, emotionally speaking. Think about using a PECS[25], which is

---

[25] The Picture Exchange Communication System or PECS is a learning system which uses visual communication aids. We'll look into it in more detail later on in this book.

no more than a drawing, used with a child who doesn't yet have that metarepresentative ability. A disaster.

You might find it very easy, but it actually isn't that obvious.

The analysis of all of these areas enables us to create a profile of the autistic person. This profile, together with the possible comorbid conditions (we can mention epilepsy in children, for example, and in adults, anxiety or depression are very common), is what will establish their level of support needs. In the end, the levels 1, 2 or 3 as regards support needs is a way of offering a 'brief guide' to locate this person at some point on the autism spectrum, as a sort of "index" which must then later be explored further.

Levels of support needs are currently used by public entities in order to determine the 'severity' or 'magnitude' of the problem and, therefore, access to therapeutic support. This means it's even more important to be very rigorous when choosing between one level or another and the need for continuous review.

Going back to those ASD diagnoses (and that's it), this breaks away from what we mentioned about diagnosing a person with ASD (without going into their support needs) as being as incorrect and incomplete as diagnosing GDD without specifying a diagnostic category.

We spoke about the importance of a label when it comes to an intervention. This is why I'm fed up of hearing other professionals say: "I don't like to give people a label" or "I don't like treating people as a group and labels are limiting". No, dear colleagues, that label sets out a path to follow, the right path, which will lead to an understanding of the unique way that person's brain works, the need to adapt to it, to later give them the necessary tools.

If you don't understand the fact that there are different ways of perceiving reality, we're done here. If you think that the normotypical way of doing things is the only right way and that everyone else needs conversion therapy, please don't work with neurodivergent people. Any health professional, especially if they work in mental health, should know that both anxiety and depression are symptoms that almost always mask something else. It's rare that these are experienced in isolation.

In January 2020 I posted the following on Twitter, and I still firmly believe in it: "Autism is a divergence in perception. Reality is perceived differently, neither better nor worse, differently. If you can't understand that, then you can't understand an autistic person, let alone help them".

Tweet[26] by @dmillanlopez. Autism understood as a form of neurodivergence.

Tips

If you're thinking about a diagnosis, here are some of my recommendations.

Complete one of the screening questionnaires you can find at the end of this book, whether the diagnosis is for you as an adult, or for a younger family member. These can give you an initial idea if you suspect autism, Asperger's syndrome, ASD, ASC, or whatever you prefer to call it. If you receive a 'concerning' result, you should think about discussing this with professionals. You can also find other questionnaires on the following website: www.espectroautista.info.

---

[26] Autism is a divergence in PERCEPTION. Reality is perceived differently – neither better nor worse. Differently. If you can't understand that, then you can't understand an autistic person, let alone help them.

What professional should you choose? Given the nature of the condition, and although it may seem obvious, you should choose someone with experience, and if possible, someone who has worked with all types of autistic people across different age groups. It might seem obvious, but experience makes such a difference.

Another important thing to note is that you must feel comfortable with the person who is going to assess you or your relative. The diagnostic process requires you to be completely open, so you must feel as though you're in a safe and secure environment. Today, many professionals within the field of autism have social media profiles and we can be watched from afar. Spend some time looking for the right person: read their posts, and if they upload videos, make sure you watch these carefully. It's very important that they're up-to-date and have a good grasp of the concept of neurodivergence.

Regarding the legal side of things, and before you embark on the process, they should give you a data protection declaration to sign, as well as an assessment agreement. The latter isn't mandatory, but they should at least let you know how they'll proceed in terms of confidentiality in order to undertake the assessment. They should also inform you of the process that will be followed. Of course, they should be a registered professional; their professional registration number is the only quick and effective way of ensuring this person has the qualification that enables them to assess you. Today, as there are intruders in all healthcare areas, this information is fundamental. Put simply, significant life experience with autism is not sufficient. They must have adequate tools and qualifications. 20,000 followers on Instagram means nothing. In fact, if this person were to undertake an intervention or assessment, not only are they a fraud, they're also committing a crime, no matter how good their intentions are.

Don't trust 'express' diagnoses. Making a correct diagnosis, under the assumption that there's already a good therapeutic relationship, shouldn't take any less than 8 hours and, of course, these should be split across several sessions to give you a break. Neuropsychological assessments tend to be gruelling. For people on the spectrum, they're generally incredibly overwhelming. Autistic people often need a few days or more to recover from the cognitive and emotional exhaustion it can cause. When I hear about assessments that have been undertaken in one afternoon, and in children, I'm left totally perplexed. The accounts of how these have been undertaken are Dantesque[27].

When it comes to minors, I tend to dedicate on average 2 hours to connect with them before even starting the different tests. A psychometric scale alone can take several hours. I'm not sure if other professionals are able to multiply spacetime, but I'm yet to work out how to do it (irony). You need to undertake a series of standardised tests to assess all the areas I've mentioned in this chapter, as well as collating all the information you can about their background. Doing all of this correctly takes time. You can't rush through it, especially if we take into account that breaks between sessions are a must, as I mentioned earlier.

I should make clear that there's no one autism diagnosis test. A diagnosis is made by comparing the results of the tests undertaken with the person's background. However, the most stan-

---

[27] Something that causes shock or horror. It is used for the reference to hell in Dante's *Divine Comedy*.

dard test today is the ADI-R (Autism Diagnostic Interview – Revised) and the ADOS-2 (Autism Diagnosis Observation Schedule). The first is simply a semi-structured interview conducted with parents (yes, parents), and is used when assessing children; I'm sure that's enough for you to imagine how (in)valid it is for an adult. The latter, as its name suggests, is a very brief observation overview designed for children from 12 months, to adults. Different studies have shown that it's totally ineffective in girls (Kenyon, 2004; Holliday-Willey, 2014; Baldwin and Costley, 2015), and especially in women. We're therefore faced with the fact that this tool was used to detect possible cases of autism in girls, they didn't detect them (Rivet and Matson, 2001), and they then received a late autism diagnosis (generally in adulthood).

This is where a common variable in autism assessment tools comes into play: they're designed using almost exclusively male samples. Today, we know that autism manifests very differently in women than it does in men[28], which is why specific tools are required for them. Among other authors, Simon Baron-Cohen and Francesca Happé are working on developing tests for the female population, which we hope will be released very soon.

---

[28] In 2010, Rudy Simone, an author self-diagnosed with Asperger's, proposed a series of diagnostic criteria to diagnose women, which was very different to those we can find in the DSM or ICD.

Very attractive material from the ADOS-2. Image by TEA Ediciones.

I've always thought of the ADOS and ADI as very limited tools. In fact, I don't generally use them, only in part or when required by an official organisation (for example, for the international validation of some of my diagnoses). They're normally used by professionals almost exclusively for a diagnostic assessment (without undertaking any other tests), which I consider reckless. The tools themselves (well, their creators) highlight that they're to be used as a complement to a more in-depth assessment.

Some examiners don't explain the tests they're going to do in any detail, keeping this information to themselves and leaving the examinee with a sense of perplexity and ignorance. It's true that on some occasions, giving an extensive explanation can have a negative predisposition, and thus condition the result of the test. Wherever possible, we should always explain exactly what we're doing and why.

What are my assessments like? Well, it depends on the person I'm assessing, but a systematic process must be followed when undertaking a differential assessment. In adults, I often 'disprove a hypothesis': sometimes an adult comes in for a consultation *convinced* they're autistic (having looked online) and is essentially looking for official confirmation. It's especially in these cases where I'll almost certainly disprove that hypothesis. On the contrary, if you go looking for confirmation, you'll most certainly find it (as we've seen previously).

The clinical assessment rules require me to assess symptoms. However, we're undertaking a differential analysis with a series of disorders: mental disorders, as referred to in the DSM manual. In the case of autism (and in other conditions), this vision, based exclusively on symptoms, is unfair to say the least; we're talking about a form of neurodivergence, about a different perspective of reality. As is the case with all humans, there are weaknesses, moments of frailty, but also strengths and significant achievements. In ASD, there's often more information for the diagnosis than analysis where the errors are (and even why). As is the case in those contexts where the autistic person 'fails' upon interacting with their surroundings, there are many other contexts where the autistic person performs excellently. So, shouldn't we be analysing them? Why is it that when we're talking about hyperfocus it normally gives an explanation based on what is 'lost' instead of 'gained' through it? These abilities are often more important when it comes to making a clinical diagnosis than the symptoms themselves, which, generally, are no more than the result of defective interaction with the surroundings on both parts (autistic person and their surroundings), as both are responsible for 50%.

A correct autism assessment should evaluate the areas I mentioned at the beginning of this chapter, using a series of standardised tools. Occasionally, other, non-standardised tools are used to compare and contrast results, but these are tools used frequently by the assessor and they can provide significant information. On that note, all the tests that offer a numeric result make me feel uneasy. All the information collected during the test is generally overlooked, and we're just left with that number which, in addition to being dangerous, can also lead to significant misinterpretation.

For example, let's use one of the tests where it's clear that only taking the number into account is a serious error and, unfortunately, is very common. The IQ test (Intelligence Quotient) on the Weschler scales. The Weschler scale of intelligence and its variants for adults and children is one of the most standardised tests used to measure intelligence worldwide. These are overused both in clinical and educational environments. Logically, the results correction is included in the manual. In order to calculate the total IQ, the value that indicates the level of intelligence of the person who has undergone the test, a series of requirements should be met, including the requirement for scores to be uniform. There cannot be significant differences between the various subscales. So, what about autism? It's the complete opposite. In general, in Asperger-type profiles, the verbal scale is far superior to the manipulative, and in Kanner-type profiles the complete opposite occurs. This brings me to make another reflection: do they really use a verbal scale to measure the intelligence of a non-verbal person?

Going back, the total IQ obtained, which often determines the support or therapeutic orientation someone receives, is incorrect. There are many cases of people diagnosed as being intellectually gifted but in reality, they're autistic and have an 'uninterpretable' IQ due to an error upon correcting the test. On the other hand, as I mentioned, the majority of the time, this final number is what we hold onto, omitting all the information that this test can give us when it comes to autism, such as processing speed, working memory, literality (yes, that too), etc.

In addition to the psychometric test which is fundamental in terms of determining the way someone processes information (beyond the IQ as we've seen), tests need to be performed in order to assess communicative and symbolic functions.

Clinical reconstruction is of utmost importance. I've already explained that establishing a good therapeutic relationship is fundamental in order to obtain all the important data regarding someone's background. That's why I'm always perplexed when I see assessments that just dive straight into the anamnesis section. Doing this interview with the parents as part of the first step of an assessment for a child is one thing, but with an adult, of all things you could do, would you really start with the most intimate part of the assessment?

> WELCOME, SIT DOWN AND **TELL ME ALL THE PARTS** OF YOUR LIFE YOU'RE **EMBARASSED** TO TALK ABOUT **IN PUBLIC**.
>
> AH, I'M GOING TO **RECORD THE SESSION**.
>
> *HELP ME...*

What a brilliant start...

Having completed the assessment, collected the anamnesis data, compared and contrasted the information and reached a conclusion, the clinical judgment – or diagnosis – is given. Communicating this is one of a professional's biggest responsibilities. What you say and how you say it can condition someone's life, or that of their family. This is where a prior screening for ableist[29] professionals can prevent significant suffering. I've heard such dark tales of how people on the spectrum or their parents have been given their diagnosis: from "start thinking about having another child because this one won't amount to much", "your child will never tell you

---

[29] Ableism is a form of discrimination or social prejudice against disabled people (Wikipedia).

they love you", "look for a residential home for them" (in children), to "you've got a disease and you're going to have to work really hard for the rest of your life" or "don't aim high so as not to disappoint yourself" (in adults). Then there are those who completely deny the reality of autism based on their own ignorance of the condition: "you can't be autistic because you make eye contact", "if you're autistic, I am too", "but how can you be autistic if you've got a job and a partner?".

Communicating a diagnosis should come hand in hand with an explanation of the idiosyncrasy of the autistic condition. Not only is what you experience important, but also the reasons why. It should come with an explanation of theory of mind, the symbolic area, dichotomous thinking... We need to offer resources and tools, starting with the situations that cause the most distress for each person with a diagnosis. We need to get rid of the sense of guilt:

- Get rid of it for the autistic adult who has grown up feeling as though they never fit in, that they're broken or missing something, and has been made to change throughout their life. There's nothing wrong with you, you're just different. You perceive the world differently, that's all.
- Get rid of it for families, especially mothers, who have been the victims of cruel judgement for years, such as "your child is like that because you don't love them[30]", and similar nonsense.

---

[30] The refrigerator mother theory stated that certain mothers were too busy and focused on their own personal and professional development to establish an affective relationship with their children, who became self-absorbed and suffered emotional loneliness, which was the cause of their autism.

With children, one of the most important things following a diagnosis is the adaptation of expectations in terms of their development. Autistic people have their own milestone agenda. Don't be pushy, nor passive.

Hans (Autista Anónimo - @AnonimoAutista), a brilliant activist within the autistic community, pinned the following tweet to his Twitter profile, where he focuses on sharing his experience of the autistic condition from a positive, neurodivergent perspective:

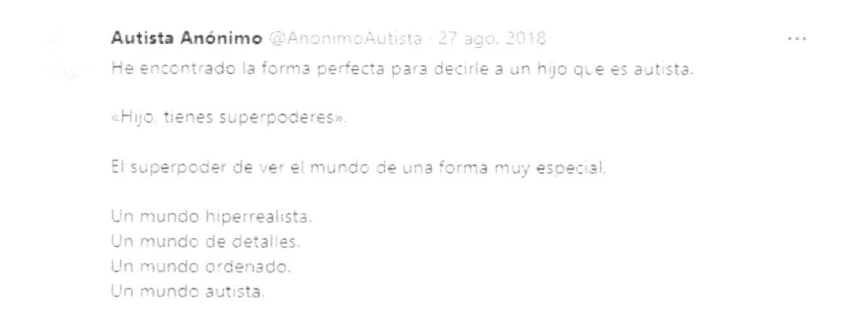

> **Autista Anónimo** @AnonimoAutista · 27 ago. 2018
> He encontrado la forma perfecta para decirle a un hijo que es autista.
>
> «Hijo, tienes superpoderes».
>
> El superpoder de ver el mundo de una forma muy especial.
>
> Un mundo hiperrealista.
> Un mundo de detalles.
> Un mundo ordenado.
> Un mundo autista.

Tweet[31] by @AnonimoAutista

In addition to offering the tools the person needs in the context in which they live their life (children in the park and at school, adults with their families, at work or in education, for example), a support system should also be put in place. Re-

---

[31] I've found the perfect way to tell a child they're autistic. You've got superpowers. Your superpower lets you see the world in a very special way.
A hyperrealist world. A detail-focused world. An ordered world. An autistic world.

gardless of whether the autistic person is an adult or if they're a loved one, similar support networks that understand how they feel, how they process information is fundamental. We need to change those unavoidable parallels drawn between your behaviour or your child with similar processing models.

The autistic community offers extraordinary support, especially in the early days following the initial impact of a diagnosis. Everyone processes things differently, but being backed by a community that gives support, understanding and advice is crucial. Whether the diagnosis gives a sense of liberation, is seen as something positive (as is the case with most adults), or if it comes as a shock (this can be the case for parents that weren't expecting it or who have a very limited, stereotypical and negative view of autism), having people who perceive the world like you or your loved one is irreplaceable.

In Spain and Latin American, the autistic community is particularly active on Twitter. You can find them by using the hashtags #SoyAutista or #AutistasResponden (the internationally-used hashtag is #ActuallyAutistic). If you're an autistic person, you're probably already following lots of people with the same condition. If you're a loved one, what are you waiting for?[32]

I posted this on Twitter in October 2020:

> I've been in this profession for 20 years, working with people on the spectrum. I've been a carer, attended camps, done therapy, diagnostic assessments, taught classes and led master's qualification in autism. I've worked alongside doctors, psychiatrists, neurologists... I've given talks at universities and hospi-

---

[32] Colloquial expression. In this context it means that you should carry out a specific action.

tals. I've led sessions with parents, a special education centre, a day care centre and a residential centre. I've designed tools for paediatricians undertaking pioneering interventions in Spain. I've managed more than 50 people in an autism centre: carers, speech therapists, physiotherapists, psychologists, special education teachers, music therapists… I've read and spoken to many of the great authors and professionals within the field of autism around the world. I've listened to and given a wide range of support to many families. And after all that, do you know who has taught me the most? Autistic people themselves. I've learned from their experiences and their perception of reality. Of their life. That's why I'm asking you, as parents of young children with ASD, to please listen to the autistic community. To autistic adults who tell things from their perspective. They can show you pathways you won't believe. Take advantage.

Chapter 5

Autism and processing

"Sometimes I lose track of time and I can spend hours on end writing code. I'm very good at it. But don't ask me to make a coffee and a slice of toast at the same time: both will be missing something, whether that's sugar, butter…" (Mario, 28 years old).

Almost all the theories that explain how the autistic brain works, even when they are written from a constructive perspective, speak of "weak connections" between different parts of the brain, or "limited development" between the different information processing centres (Nason, 2020).

According to Bill Nason[33]: "Autism is a series of information processing differences that change the way in which information is registered, integrated and absorbed (2020)". Of course, it's a difference when compared to how a neurotypical would process this. This doesn't mean it's a defect or a problem, it's just different to normative processing, as we'll see here.

---

[33] Bill Nason is a mental health professional who specialises in people with behavioural difficulties. He is very well-known for leading the Facebook page *Autism Discussion Page*.

From this theoretical construct, which I'm very much in agreement with (with certain nuances I'll go into later), there are two general processes that characterise the processing pathway of an autistic brain.

1) Difficulty processing multiple signals, stimulants or information adequately.

2) Processing delay.

However, in our society, the demand tends to be the opposite, to the detriment of people on the spectrum. Let's take a common, necessary event in our society as an example: social interactions. Specifically, we're talking about a conversation.

1) At the same time as listening to what the other person is saying, we have to be aware of their body language, facial expressions, and everything that has to do with non-verbal communication (NVC).

2) We also have to take into account the context in which the interaction takes place. Each context has a series of rules, which don't tend to be written down and are just 'assumed' by neurotypical people.

3) While we're listening to what they're saying, we have to simultaneously formulate and prepare our response or contributions to the conversation.

4) And, when it's our turn to speak (it's often unclear when this is), we must pay attention to the feedback from the other person upon hearing our words. This processing is fundamental in order to achieve a real interaction that goes beyond a 'question-answer-end'

structure which often occurs in interactions with an autistic person.

5) Lastly, we must consider those more intuitive rules that allow us to start, maintain and end a conversation depending on the person, context, pace of the conversation, etc.

> YOU HAVE TO *PAY ATTENTION* TO:
> - THE VERBAL MESSAGE
> - BODY LANGUAGE (NVC)
> - CONTEXT
> - FORMULATING A RESPONSE
> - FEEDBACK
> - RULES FOR STARTING, MAINTAINING AND ENDING A CONVERSATION...

> PAY ATTENTION TO *ALL OF THIS*, AS WELL AS WHAT THEY'RE *SAYING* TO YOU.

> WTF?

A simple task...

In this context, different parts of the brain have to work and communicate effectively. This means that the brain stem, the cerebellum, the limbic system (nuclear centre for emotional processing) and the prefrontal cortex must be in continuous connection.

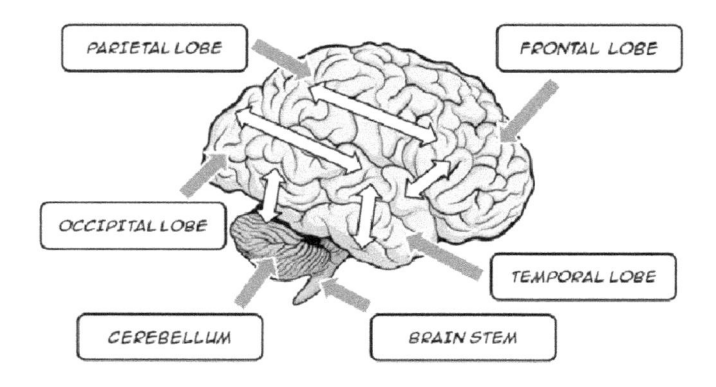

Multi-channel information processing in the brain.

In other words, a wide range of signals coming from different places need to be processed quickly (and superficially). We're talking about one-by-one. Imagine a group situation: the cognitive demand increases exponentially. Autistic people who are continually exposed to these types of demands tend to experience diverse cognitive consequences. We'll talk about autistic meltdowns, burnout and shutdowns in the next chapters.

"I prefer conversations via e-mail or WhatsApp. I don't have to be aware of whether or not the facial expressions the other person is making fit with what they're saying. When I have to do that, I get lost in what they're saying" (Carmen, 43 years old).

For Bill Nason, the autistic brain has some weak connections between the cerebral centres responsible for integrated information processing This 'weak wiring' is supported by the evidence of a greater number of neurons and larger size in certain parts of the brain that can be found in autistic people when compared to neurotypical people (Courchesne et al., 2011). This would explain the processing differences in people on the spectrum. Despite this author's good intentions, as is the case with other authors, I think this conclusion is incredibly unfair, as it only states it is a 'wrong' way of processing. At the end of the day, it's produced from a historic and social perspective in which fast (and superficial) processing of a series of information (much of which is based on inferences as opposed to realities, as we'll see later on in this book), is that which prevails in order to thrive socially. Ultimately, this completely side-lines other forms of processing.

Another way of looking at it would be to demonstrate that the autistic brain is designed for a different, more specialist purpose that requires a deep and dedicated form of processing. In order to do this, it requires brain characteristics different to those required by neurotypical people. In fact, throughout history, some societies have praised this more meticulous, detail-focused type of processing over superficial processing. Is it a coincidence that the majority of history's 'geniuses' were not particularly sociable, and were detail-oriented, dedicated and selective? Could it not be that divergent thinking, which many a time has gone against the norm, has enabled significant advances in humanity?

Bill Nason adds an interesting concept to this equation of divergent thinking in autism; static versus dynamic processing. In reality (as is the case with many new theories on autism), it's no more than a twist[34] on incredibly well-known concepts, such as invariance and desire for predictability.

---

[34] A twist is used to imply that the plot takes an unexpected turn, has a different meaning to that which is first thought.

According to Nason, it's important we differentiate between those stimuli with static information (in which the information does not vary) and those with dynamic information (and can, therefore, vary). Static information is specific, constant and absolute. For example, we have historical facts or invariable rules such as mathematics, but we also have repetitive patterns that aren't susceptible to change. Dynamic information requires continuous assessment and depends on the context. Social norms are also considered dynamic.

When it comes to static information, an autistic person can perform optimally. However, the majority of the concepts this world complies are not static. I tend to use the term 'permeable', so much so that the initial concept can be partially static, but many of the surrounding aspects are susceptible to change. In these cases, the person on the spectrum can find themselves at a disadvantage compared to a neurotypical person, who tends to take to these changeable environments like a fish to water[35].

The fact that autistic people are often more comfortable with objects than with people draws from this explanation: objects are more specific, constant and predictable than humans, who are dynamic and unpredictable. Autistic people look for invariability in themselves, which they can in fact achieve (not without making an effort), but they also look for it in their surroundings. This is a life-long, challenging, if not impossible task.

The autistic person ends up obliged to interact with a changeable and unpredictable world. 'Chaotic', in the words of some

---

[35] A non-literal expression used to refer to circumstances under which someone feels comfortable, or to which they take with ease or dexterity.

autistic people. They often fall apart: it's an exhausting and disheartening task. It's also an ungrateful task, as many of the people who surround them don't realise the incredible effort to which an autistic person goes. To the untrained eye, as is the case of the neurotypical eye, the person has a problem and a deficit they need to 'fix'.

However, if we always look for the explanation in terms of deficits, we'll never advance in terms of how we view autism. The human being tends to stigmatise and brand anything that isn't in keeping with the majority as wrong, categorising it as a disease or disorder. If you put everyone through this same judgment in terms of ability, using the same context, a person who is overqualified in that task will be victorious, merely for being overqualified in that one specific area. When put through this unfair test, all different ways of thinking and processing are condemned to failure. This is what autistic people have been subjected to for decades: if you're unable to adapt to society, I'll exclude you from it. This is all because the person has a different processing system that doesn't fit in with the way the majority processes information.

This injustice doesn't occur exclusively in autism. Something similar happens when we talk about an 'invisible' developmental condition. Nobody would expect someone on crutches to run up the stairs, but we continuously expect people on the spectrum to do something similar. And, as if that wasn't enough, we tell them that 'it can't be that bad if they do it every day', totally overlooking and shunning all the effort they've been making for years; the effort that has a series of repercussions we'll discuss below, and in the chapter on masking.

The things they say to autistic people and that really make you feel great.

And that's why the paradigm of neurodivergence in autism is so necessary. Autistic processing is the complete opposite to neurotypical processing: instead of processing in parallel, an autistic person processes sequentially (one thing after the other); and, instead of processing quickly (or superficially), the person on the spectrum undertakes a deep and dedicated analysis, which is why it's slower in comparison.

Sometimes, the way information is received is quicker than an autistic person is able to process, which results in a general loss of information (which would correlate to Uta Frith's central coherence hypothesis in autism) and the autistic person has to make an effort to make the information make sense with just the pieces they have to go on. This is where the processing delay Nason mentions comes into play, which has a variable duration (anything from 10 seconds to hours, depending on the context). What happens is, if we give enough time to receive all the information correctly, the autistic person's response tends to be correct and accurate, but if we pressure them and force them to process more quickly, it can end in disaster.

Putting children under this pressure of speed storage and recovery of information will only lead to avoidance or finding avoidance strategies such as 'no' or 'I don't know'. For adults, it can cause interaction avoidance, at least when it's face-to-face. If we think about the fact that autistic people have a marked ability to think in images (they translate everything they're told into images prior to creating a complete image and response), this processing delay can be even greater.

"I get lost in group conversations. When I want to respond, it's as if the moment has already been and gone. It makes me feel stupid, which is why I try to avoid them as much as possible" (Cris, 28 years old)

If we analyse this way of processing as tasks that require fast processing speeds, parallel tasks, tasks that require the intuition of social cues that are unclear, processing information without an ambiguous meaning, it's clear that an autistic person will generally be at a disadvantage compared to a neurotypical person.

Does that mean, for example, that an autistic person would find doing several tasks at once impossible? No, but they'll have to pay the price either way. Essentially, we're asking a brain to work at a speed and intensity for which it hasn't been designed. It's like asking a long-distance runner to do a short distance race. They'll be able to do it, but it won't be as effective as if they were to run a marathon, and they could even injure themselves if they consistently run this sort of race.

"At work, I sometimes have to do several things at once. If I make an effort, I can do it, but I'm totally exhausted for the next few days. I prefer to do tasks one by one, which is how I work best" (Rosa, 33 years old).

What happens if we turn it on its head[36]? If we think about tasks that require a deeper form of processing and detailed analysis, tasks that require us to memorise facts or proven information that is not susceptible to change, identify patterns and sequences, memorise all types of images, the use of computer equipment or tasks that require logical reasoning. Who would be at a disadvantage? Now who would appear to have a deficit?

The reality is, neither side has a deficit. They're just different ways of processing and, therefore, both have their strengths and weaknesses, depending on the context.

Tips

Whether you're autistic or have an autistic loved one, it would be a great help if you could put these pointers into practice. They're essential, at least in the autistic person's home environment. If you're an adult, ask the people around you to keep the following in mind. If you're a family member, implement these in your relationship with the person on the spectrum.

1) Use short, very specific sentences, especially when talking to an autistic child. Parents tend to say things like: we want to give them an instruction, but what we do is:

"Enrique, I've already told you, stay by my side. I can't follow your every move, so when I talk to you, I need you to listen to me, so stop now or I'm going to lose my temper with you" (María, mother to Enrique, 10 years old).

---

[36] Non-literal expression used to express the fact that something has been "turned around" or roles have been inverted.

Here, the practical thing would be to say: "Enrique, stop". Ultimately, that's what we want him to understand. Everything else is unimportant and confusing.

2) Use specific, literal language when talking to an autistic person.

"Marina, I need you to send me this piece of work, when you can"
(Marina's Manager, 35 years old)

We need to establish specific time constraints. Let's not be confusing. Ask yourself this question: Can you apply 'depends' to your instruction? If this is the case, you're doing it wrong. Be specific. We'll look into this topic further in the chapter on symbolisation.

3) Don't use insinuations when talking to a person on the spectrum. You might think it's socially convenient, but an autistic person prefers the message to be clear. Don't be afraid to be too direct.

Don't ask: "So, we'll see each other around here later then?", if what you really want to know is if the other person wants to meet up later. It's better to ask: "Do you want to meet up later?"

4) When talking to an autistic person, try to ensure what your saying has a linear structure: don't jump between topics. Start from the beginning and follow a temporal progression. Try and focus on the most important aspects, especially if there are many agents (people or characters) involved in what you're talking about.

5) Give the autistic person time to process the information they've been given, especially before moving onto another topic.

6) When it comes to children, it's particularly important to check they've understood us. Don't assume they've understood without confirmation. This is one of the most common errors in education: "There's no need, they've understood it perfectly".

7) Regardless of whether we're talking to children or adults, we need to use and demand visual aids (agendas, bimodal communication systems and written information, in addition to verbal, etc.).

Of course, these tips need to be adapted to each individual. The fact that an autistic person has a different form of processing to a neurotypical person means just that. When a neurotypical person realises they're talking to an autistic person, the most common reaction is to infantilise them, which even occurs in clinical and healthcare contexts. It's humiliating and shouldn't be tolerated.

Yeah.

Chapter 6

Attention and executive functions

"I'm dreadful at all strategy games. Well, just like at life, really". (Clara, 28 years old)

One of the greatest concerns among parents of autistic children that I work with is their child's supposed short attention span. They tend to ask me, "Daniel, how can I get my child to listen to me?" or "How can I get my child to have a longer attention span?".

In most cases, my response is unexpected. In autism, often this lack of attention is nothing more than a symptom, as opposed to being the actual cause of what's going on. As I was saying, autistic people process reality differently. This type of processing focuses on pragmatism, practicality of things, or, in other words, their use.

An autistic child is often labelled as having an attention problem, when all they're after is for what we ask them to do to make sense, or at least in their world. Important: this doesn't mean to say that there isn't in fact an attention problem, I'm just highlighting that we need to study other, more central variables (symbolic field, processing, etc.), before jumping to the conclusion that "this kid doesn't pay attention".

Experience shows us that if we create a structured environment, with predictable people and surroundings, as well as working on tasks with a functional purpose with autistic kids, this supposed lack of attention is significantly reduced, or perhaps even disappears. If we ensure the activity makes sense and we're still seeing inattentive behaviour patterns, then we can focus on analysing this attention deficit.

> "The relationship between the construct of attention and the construct of executive functioning is rather blurry and overlaps. Identifying which are the executive functions is very complex, so much so that the majority include them in other functions" (Onandia, 2019).

This reflection by my colleague Iban Onandia is a determining factor in the case of autism. Just as we cannot assume a lack of attention in autism without establishing other key points first, such as the meaning of the activity, nor can we do so without taking into account executive functions.

The hypothesis of executive functions in autism (Pennington and Ozonoff, 1996) is one of the most scientifically-proven theories and is very much a 'favourite' among neuropsychologists. However, there's a strong biological component which makes this plausible, far from psychological constructs that are no more than that: constructs with no physical entity to support them, or at least, without an entity as clear as the frontal lobes.

Without going too far into this explanatory model, the hypothesis is based on the observation of symptoms in autistic people, compared to people who have suffered prefrontal lobe lesions. Other authors (Damaso and Maurer, 1978) had already begun thinking about this hypothesis a few decades prior.

What would the loss of or alterations in executive functions imply? Among other abilities, executive functions play a part in our:

1) Ability to plan: from constructing a meaningful, coherent argument, without making jumps, to undertaking an activity or task consisting of independent parts.

2) Cognitive flexibility: the ability to quickly modify our prior criteria based on new information in order to find an alternative different to that which we found initially.

3) Working memory: parallel storage of varied information, separating that which is relevant from that which is irrelevant (see previous chapter).

4) Monitoring: a parallel process (again) that enables the anticipation of the consequence of the action process prior to completing the action.

5) Ability to inhibit: interruption of automatic responses produced by the input of new information.

PLANNING

COGNITIVE FLEXIBILITY

WORKING MEMORY

MONITORING

INHIBITION ABILITY

PROCESSING SPEED

ATTENTION CONTROL

PROACTIVITY

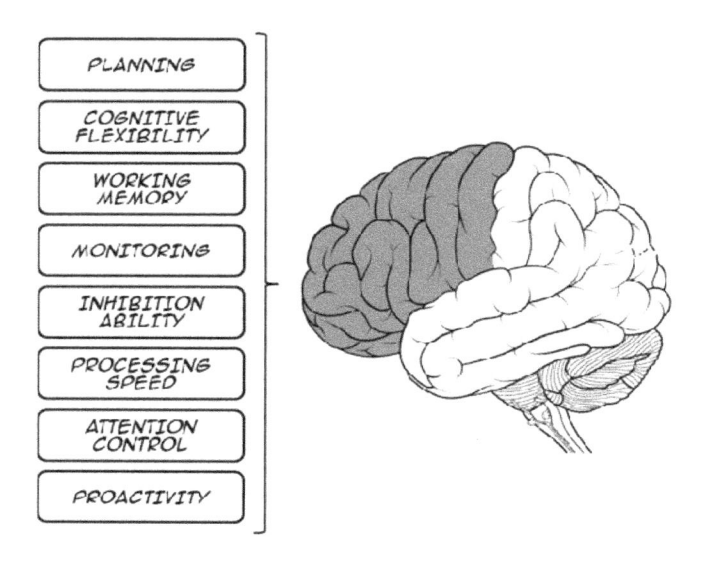

Prefrontal lobe and executive functions.

Executive function:

> […] is the cognitive construct used to describe behaviour with the aim of achieving an objective, oriented towards the future, which are considered mediated by the frontal lobes. These include planning, inhibition of overbearing responses, flexibility, organised search and working memory. All of the executive function behaviour shares the need to disconnect from the immediate surroundings or external context to guide the action through mental models or internal representations (Ozonoff et al., 1994).

With this in mind, together with what we've already seen in the previous chapter on information processing in autism, it doesn't seem as though this explicative model fits in badly with the autistic cognition, but where are the symbolic difficulties or all the problems as a result of emotional processing?

It was clear that this proposal was insufficient in order to describe the full nature of people on the spectrum, which is why the theory of executive function began to be combined with theory of mind (see chapter 9) and the studies of emotional perception, in order to offer a more inclusive explicative model for autism (Ozonoff et al. 1991). The result of this research appeared to conclude that autistic people not only have a deficit in executive functions but, beyond the behavioural level, there were also cognitive alterations, such as:

- Anticipation difficulties.
- Lack of activity monitoring.
- Inhibition difficulties.
- Lack of proactivity and difficulties in terms of looking to the future.

Are the supposed executive functioning issues idiosyncratic characteristics of this condition? We already de-mystified this in chapter 4. There are a myriad of disorders and conditions that demonstrate a significant presence of symptoms linked to executive functions. Besides injuries caused by accidents and illnesses that lead to cognitive deterioration, we can also mention bipolar disorder, manic-depressive disorder, obsessive compulsive disorder, and of course, attention deficit disorder (ADD) and attention hyperactivity deficit disorder (ADHD).

It comes as no surprise that autism, Level 1 or Asperger's, are often confused and overlap with ADHD, and one of the key symptoms they share are alterations in executive functions, although that isn't the only one. To name just a few, we can also mention certain language alterations (prosodic anomalies and pragmatic alterations), recurring interest in different topics and issues with social interaction.

On the other hand, there are certain aspects that differ between these conditions, such as: in autism, attention deficit is more linked to a difficulty in terms of understanding and interacting in social situations, whereas in ADHD there is a more generalised attention deficit. In autism on the other hand, in terms of difficulties encountered in social relationships, these are determined by a very complex casuistry that in terms of its symptoms presents as a lack of social skills. In ADHD, behaviour that can at times be very disruptive due to its impulsive nature predominates. Lastly, despite hyperfocus being present in both cases, "[…] it appears to be more directed and more productive in autism than in ADHD" (Onandia, 2020). Could this be linked to the idiosyncrasies of recurrent interests in autism?

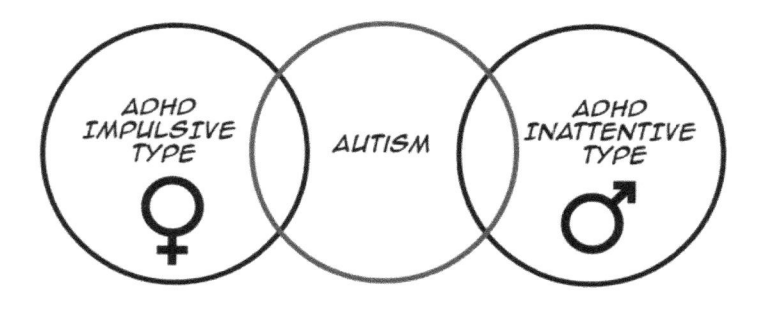

Autism and ADHD in females and males.

The old version of the DSM did not allow a joint autism and ADHD diagnosis. Fortunately, this was changed with the DSM5, as there are many cases in which both conditions present in the same person, thus resulting in a combined diagnosis (Gjevik et al., 2011). The pattern in males tends to be a combination of autism and ADHD, inattentive sub-type, and in females it tends to be autism with ADHD, hyperactive sub-type, similar to the prevalence of ADHD when it is diagnosed without an ADHD diagnosis (Medici, 2018).

So, is there an attention deficit present in autism? Even when we could disconnect attention from other cognitive processes, the studies undertaken to date are (surprise, surprise[37]), inconclusive. A study by Juan Martos (2008) concluded that determined attention-related process such as selective[38] or sustained attention appear to not only be altered in autism, but sometimes they obtain significant results in different tests, when compared to neurotypical samples. Is that surprising? If you've been paying attention while reading both this chapter and the previous one, it shouldn't be: these processes require an ability to concentrate and process without changing the focus. This can lead to good performance if your brain processes sequentially and has the ability to hyperfocus. However, it does appear that there are difficulties upon examination of processes such as split and joint attention. These are processes that require parallel processing and have both a social component and in terms of the purpose of the activity.

Independently of the possibility to consider attention skills in people on the spectrum as something relevant and separate from executive functions, it's clear that there's a need to evaluate these in terms of their importance in terms of the evolution of autistic kids and adults, as I mentioned in chapter 4.

---

[37] Ironic expression. In this case it implies that there really is no surprise at all.
[38] Selective attention, also known as focused attention, refers to the ability to focus the mind on a specific stimulus or task, despite the presence of other environmental stimuli.

In order to do this, several different materials with standardised tests are used, such as: BRIEF-2, TESEN, ANILLAS test, FDT, ENFEN, and the famous Wisconsin card classification test (WCST), among others.

To give me an initial idea, I generally use the Tower of Hanoi.

The Tower of Hanoi. Giving autistic people nightmares since 1883.

The Tower of Hanoi is a puzzle or maths-based game invented by French mathematician Edouard Lucas in 1883. This one-player game consists of a number disks with a circular hole in the middle, that are stacked by placing them on one of the three posts fixed to a board. The aim of the game is to move the pile to one of the other posts, following certain rules, such as a bigger disk cannot be placed on top of a smaller disk. So, why is this such a fantastic game to test executive functions? The rules are incredibly simple, but the involvement of all the processes that highlight executive functions are put to the test right from the start: the need to plan, otherwise you'll find yourself stuck after just a few moves. You need to vary your strategy frequently: what works at the beginning might not be useful later on. You need to think beyond your next move, considering the mid-term consequences of your decisions. Finally, you need to monitor your actions as you make your moves.

Of course, this game and the standardised tests are no more than just approximations as to how executive functions operate in each person. Only the analysis of real situations can give us a reliable sample of their implication in the life of each person.

Tips

In autism, executive functions are intrinsically linked to another series of processes we've seen, such as sequential processing, among others, such as polarised thinking, symbolic processes and mentalist processes (later on in this book).

As I highlighted at the beginning of this chapter, in children, intervention should be based on giving meaning to the activity we're asking them to complete. Once this premise has been established, the intervention can begin by designing strategies. These strategies should be both external (structuring the environment, giving visual aids, structuring time…), which are those established by parents or teachers, and internal for the child (self-instructions, internal feedback). Ultimately, the application of the TEACCH structured teaching method.

The TEACCH methodology (Treatment and Education of Autistic and related Communication-handicapped Children) was created by Eric Schopler in the late 1960s. This methodology was aimed at autistic people of all types and ages. The authors focused more on studies in childhood, but there was a reason for this. The key objective established by Schopler was the prevention of the unnecessary institutionalisation in assistance centres at the time, and 'prevention' was therefore fundamental. The methodology is based, essentially, on anticipating time, space and agents (other people) for autistic people, at all times. Ultimately, complete structure via visual anticipation mechanisms.

One of the biggest challenges that put children's (and older) executive functions to the test are long-cycle tasks or those that are divided into small subtasks. In these cases (following the paradigm of the TEACCH methodology), visual sequencing of these tasks is very useful, as is the creation of a timeline that enables external monitoring of the activity until the objective is completed.

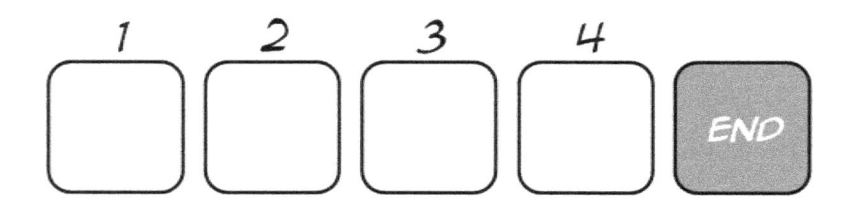

WE PLAN BY ESTABLISHING AN ORDER WITH A CLEAR START AND FINISH AND SUPERVISE EXECUTION (MONITORING)

Sequential task planning and supervision, always with an end goal.

One of the significant difficulties is the ability to synthesise information. It's very common for students on the spectrum to end up highlighting almost everything when they're asked to highlight the most important information in a text. Or when they have to do an outline or summary, they end up transcribing all the content from the original text straight into their notes. To be able to work on this, it's important to take advantage of the strengths in autism. First and foremost, they must understand the information, organise it, select the most important parts and generate their own explanation of it.

On my YouTube channel you can find a video where one of the autistic young people I work with created his own visual scheme to be able to study a history topic at college.

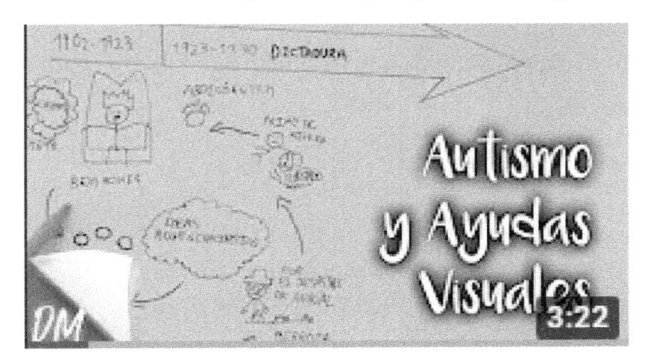

Using strengths in autism.

Another challenge that arises comes as a result of the difficulties encountered when it comes to generalising learning or creating different alternatives to solve the same problem. Once an itinerary has been learned, it's hard to offer an alternative: why offer an alternative if the existing one already works? This process, depending on the desire of invariance, can lead to cognitive inflexibility and an obstacle in terms of learning to use other tools that can be applied to other contexts. This is why we should alternate these challenges in order to produce a repertoire of varied tools that will help them resolve diverse problems (self-management, autonomy, communication, learning, socialising...).

Generally speaking, time management poses a huge challenge for people on the spectrum. For starters, in children, the concept of time alone is something relatively complex and that requires continuous learning. When a neurotypical person has generalised their learning, they start to use it in a non-literal way. For a person on the spectrum, however, the non-specific nature of time and waiting are a potential source of anxiety, regardless of their age. If expressions such as 'wait a moment' can cause anxiety for autistic adults, imagine the effect this could have on a child for whom the concept of time is unclear and who doesn't have a mechanism of anticipation to help them during this waiting time.

So, what can we do then? Again, we'll use visual mechanisms of anticipation, especially if we're talking about children with difficulties understanding. If they still don't understand the concept of time and the use of clocks to tell time, we should make one they *can* understand, even though we have to calculate the time ourselves. At the end of the day, it's likely what they need to know is when a wait begins or ends, and be able to see how the time left until the objective is 'consumed'. Using the concept of a sand timer we can modify depending on the circumstances. I propose a system similar to the one you can see in this photo.

A multipurpose visual "clock"

With this panel, on which we can move the arrow as the waiting time progresses, for example (it doesn't matter if this is 5, 10 or 30 minutes), the child can see how this waiting time is 'ending' and consequently control their anxiety and they don't have to suffer due to the unpredictable nature of the wait.

If we're clear as to which time period we're establishing (and knowing that this isn't going to vary), we can use a different system such as the Time-timer. This is a visual timer very similar to a kitchen timer. You can programme a red band which shows the amount of time you want to select. Once set up, the red line on the time starts to disappear, little by little. This enables external monitoring and an anticipated end at all times.

Often, when it comes to anticipation strategies, emphasis is placed on showing the start of the activity. However, we forget about a differential aspect, such as showing the end. This is also a must for autistic adults.

"Every time I used to go out with my family it was agony. Now we establish an end to these trips. Just knowing that there was an end reduced my

anxiety and I could finally start enjoying the activity, even if it went on for a bit longer in the end" (Marc, 25 years old).

In order to improve planning skills in children, and given the well-known generalisation difficulties, I recommend two types of intervention: one direct and one indirect. The direct includes mechanisms such as training in self-instruction, task lists and creating mental maps. On the other hand, the indirect route includes using board games as strategies to practice planning.

There are thousands or board games. To just name a few: *Virus, Ticket to ride* or other more classic games such as *Othello*. In general, any non-linear game in which your actions have long-term consequences and during which you have to follow the game and the other players will work for this purpose. Some computer games I'd recommend are graphic point-and-click adventures, such as *Secret of Monkey Island, Broken Sword, Loom* or *Gibbous – A Cthulhu Adventure*. For mobile devices I'd definitely recommend the *Monument Valley* saga.

Wonderful in every way © UstwoGames.

In adults, the work is generally focused on being able to establish anticipation and planning mechanisms adapted to each person. But the key remains the same: this anticipation must be visual and permanent, or at least quickly and easily accessible.

The story of the two autistic adults I work with tends to be very similar to that of the parents when I'm so insistent on anticipation. The adults tend to show certain resistance when it comes to applying these measures. They tend to say: "Is a calendar with all my activities, even the routine ones, really going to have a positive impact?". But if they overcome this initial resistance, the final response tends to be something like (as is the case with parents when they do the same for their children): "I can't believe it. It's totally changed things".

Your autistic brain needs routines and planning: listen to it and give it what it asks for. There are already enough external events we can't control. Unpredictable events that challenge our structure and stability. We should give ourselves a safe space where we can undertake our activities, whether they be personal, academic or work-focused, in an environment in which we can control as many variables as possible. Control as much as you can. Neurotypical people live happily with unpredictability and total spontaneity, uncertainty or, they can at least develop compensation strategies very quickly. People on the spectrum have their strengths elsewhere. It's not a problem, but don't compare yourself with something that is the complete opposite to you.

Using outlines like mental maps, cause and effect diagrams or Venn diagrams[39] can be useful in cases where thought proc-

---

[39] Venn diagrams are frameworks used in set theory, popular in mathematics, class logic and diagrammatic reasoning.

esses become confusing (often those related to social relationships or emotional comprehension) or very polarised and categoric (due to dichotomous thinking, see the following chapter), and the processes related to executive functions are a hindrance when it comes to understanding and confronting certain situations. Even though from my perspective I'd recommend you put the content of these thoughts on paper to avoid recurrent looping thoughts, often difficulties with information synthesis can turn the potential solution into a problem in the form of a piece of paper with too much information written on it.

At the end of the day, everyone (both autistic and neurotypical people) uses anticipation mechanisms because, otherwise what is the calendar we've got on our phone or computer? We all need anticipation, it's just that autistic people need more. Significantly so. Some people on the spectrum find making these plans and lists incredible satisfying: the world, which is incredibly unstructured, absurd and unpredictable, suddenly makes sense. Or at least in the case of this little area over which they have certain control.

"I think I'd be happy in prison; you know. Strict schedules for activities, lights, clothes, no variations whenever someone sees fit. You always know what you're going to be doing at all times, every single day. Uncertainty would be minimal; everything would be predictable. Amazing. (Laura, 25 years old).

Chapter 7

Dichotomous thinking

"He's not my friend anymore, which makes him my enemy" (Jaime, 12 years old)

The reality of autism is so broad, rich and breath-taking that at times, regardless of how much you've read or studied, you don't really see the true dimension of this rich and unique condition until you've come across it.

There's a moment I remember as if it were yesterday: when the dichotomous way people on the spectrum process emotions became clear to me. Polarised or dichotomous thinking (Ellis, 1962) is a unique autistic characteristic. It's true that autism isn't the only condition in which this way of thinking occurs, but its unique in its nature.

Dichotomous thinking has been very closely linked to different pathologies as an 'erroneous' way of thinking. In fact, it was part of Albert Ellis' cognitive distortions and was mentioned in Beck's cognitive therapy (1979) as a 'symptom' occurring in anxiety, depression, obsessive compulsive disorder (DSM axis I) and those defined as personality disorders (DSM axis II), such as paranoid personality disorder, borderline personality disorder, etc. I'm sure that this will ring a bell[40] for many people on the spectrum who happen to be reading this. It's not a coincidence that many people with autistic spectrum condition also have the comorbid conditions described in axis I and may have even received incorrect diagnoses included in axis II. The importance of a differential diagnosis is crucial in terms of avoiding these huge blunders that can have such a negative impact on somebody's life. The big issue in terms of diagnosis based on symptoms is the following: not going any further and discovering the nature of these symptoms, as we saw earlier in the chapter on the diagnosis of autism.

When I was director of the autism centre in Badajoz, we offered a service similar to early intervention (from the age of 6 up) called functional rehabilitation, where we worked with young people on the spectrum who attended mainstream school and who did therapy once a week at our centre. We had a huge number of young people, but they all fit into two similar age groups. Unlike what had been done previously, I decided to do something that felt logical, but something that nobody in Spain appeared to be doing: if one of the main challenges these young people faced was making friends, why on earth weren't we offering group therapy with their peers? Now it seems very much a Captain Obvious[41] situation, but at the time, therapy was viewed even more strictly than it is now: "go to therapy, learn how to do things with an adult in an unwelcoming, cold room and then transfer this knowledge into your day-to-day life". Besides being completely inappropriate, in almost all conditions, it's practically therapeutic suicide for autistic people due to their generalisation difficulties (Baer, 1977).

---

[40] Non-literal expression that implies you know something or it's familiar.
[41] Captain Obvious is used to refer to a self-obvious truth.

Before taking the plunge[42] and angering the ringleaders, I decided to get an opinion from my colleagues. I called María Llorente, psychologist specialised in autism, with whom I'd worked at Deletrea, and she thought it was a wonderful idea. We both agreed that they needed to be split into groups according to their level of "functioning" and that all (or none) of them were aware of their diagnosis. And that's what we did. We created two groups of younger people, between 10 and 13 years old, and another, older group, which, coincidently, included two women (women with Asperger's syndrome, at the time.)

Anyway, I'm going off on one[43]. So, there was a boy in the kids' group, let's call him Pedro, who appeared particularly 'full on'. He appeared very 'functional', but he needed a lot of anticipation. I worked with him individually, and he also took part in the group sessions. In these sessions, we used one of the multi-purpose rooms in the building. It had several big, colourful armchairs. On day one, Pedro came into the room and said: "I love the green armchair. Eugh, I hate the red armchair!". Naturally, the first thing that comes to mind is 'he's so dramatic'. So, I intervened with my infamous tact, grabbed him by the T-shirt and said: "Don't worry, sit on your favourite one, it's far away from the red one". And that was that. Within a few seconds the boy was laughing and I managed to get rid of that feeling that appeared to have got him 'stuck' at the beginning of the session. We then started the group session with the other boys. I kept looking over at Pedro out the corner of

---

[42] Non-literal expression used to refer to taking the risk and trying something new, unknown or something we cannot fully understand or control. However, it can bring us a either significant achievement or be our biggest downfall.

[43] Non-literal expression used when someone is going off-topic or diverging from their original conversation topic.

my eye, because something was up: he was fidgeting in the armchair and it was clear he wasn't paying attention. Was he looking at his peer sat in the red armchair? Or at the armchair itself?

On the left: extreme emotional intensity

I decided to take him out of the room and when he calmed down, I began to talk to him about it. He said: "I can't avoid it, I want to break it because I hate it, and when you hate something, you have to destroy it". It was clear that he wasn't faking it, he wasn't making a scene just to get out of the activity which, he happened to love. It was a real, genuine feeling, or at least for him. And that's the most important part.

I started to look up some references so I knew how to address the issue and, of course, I also spoke to his mum, whom he lived with. The little I found spoke of the cliché of supposed emotional dysregulation in autism[44]. In theory, it could be that, but why is this dysregulation always present in extreme emotions? Shouldn't this be the case at all times if this dysregulation does in fact exist? Pedro's fixation on routines and his

---

[44] There is no professional consensus as to whether or not emotional dysregulation exists in autism.

clearly dichotomous thinking gave me the answer: in a world in which you experience everything in black and white, 'black & white thinking' (Fairbairn, 1939), isn't it logical that you experience emotions in the same way?

I put my theory to the test and the pieces appeared to fit: Pedro expressed himself with intensities that appeared exaggerated, not just when he was angry or sad, but also when he experienced positive emotions. When even the tiniest of things made him feel happy, Pedro was absolutely euphoric: when we read the comic he liked, he would literally jump around the room for joy. If he found a coin on the floor, he just couldn't stop jumping. When he was going on holiday, he expressed himself in this exact same way. Of course, in a joyful situation, we all love seeing a super happy child and, even though this behaviour seems a bit over the top, it isn't seen as something dysfunctional. This, however, wasn't the case if sad news or a sad event plunged him into what appeared to be depression and uncontrollable sobbing. He doesn't appear to regulate his emotions now, does he?

So, how do we work on this? All the situations that always led him to feel incredibly polarised emotions, and he didn't appear to be able to rank these feelings depending on the situation that had provoked it. I remember he said to me:

- *The thing is, Daniel, there are things that make me feel very happy, and others that make me so angry. Is that bad?*
- *Of course not, it happens to me too. Sometimes I feel incredibly angry, just like you. Other times I feel a bit angry, but that feeling goes away in no time.*
- *I don't know how to do that.*

We started to make a list of situations that had made him angry. Every single one of them caused a similar reaction: very intense and persistent. I thought that maybe he could tell me which one had made him the angriest and which one the least, but it was impossible. They all were equally as intense. He was unable to rank them according to intensity. This was when I remembered the 'first commandment' of autism: visual aids, at all times. I wrote down the situations he had described on six different cards. This is when things started to change:

"Mmm, thinking about it, I'd say this one here, well, I think this is the one that makes me the angriest. If that happens to me, I completely lose it. But this one makes me very angry, but less angry than the other one".

At least we'd now established the most intense and the least intense. We started to try and put the next ones in order, and little by little he managed it. We put them in order of intensity: from the least intense to the most intense. This is when a truly complex variable came into play, because how do you explain to a kid that his way of thinking and feeling isn't bad, but that experiencing everything so intensely can be very frustrating and painful for him? Pedro decided to set the pace himself:

"Now we've put everything in order, we can assign them a colour because I feel emotions as colours, and when I get angry, I see everything in red".

Today, it's very common to associate synaesthesia with autism[45]. It's not a characteristic that is always seen in this condition, but when it does, its presentation tends to be homogeneous, without the variety found on the spectrum. Some people see numbers as different colours or shapes, depending on

---

[45] Synaesthesia is a non-pathological variation of human perception. Synaesthetic people automatically and involuntarily experience the activation of an additional sensory or cognitive channel in response to specific stimuli.

whether they're odd or even. Others feel a specific sensation in a given part of their body when they smell a certain smell. I'll go into more detail on this in chapter 11.

Let's go back to Pedro.

"So, colours? – I said -. How about we draw a thermometer, because when you get angry it's as if the temperature is increasing?"

He really liked that idea, so I said we'd work on that in our next session. Now you can Google "emotional thermometer" and get thousands of results pop up. Back in the ISDN[46] days, when you would send an email and just have to deal with it. I don't know if Photoshop had been invented at this point and, although I could have drawn it by hand, I decided to use Microsoft Word autoshapes, and this is the result.

This is the emotional thermometer (based on the work of Attwood, 2002) that I made for Pedro, and I still use it. In fact, you can find this same image on websites and blogs around the world, who have used it at my discretion. *Mea culpa*[47] for not having added a watermark (only joking).

---

[46] ISDN internet connection. The Integrated Services Digital Network (ISDN) is a standard network system for data transmission via copper telephone wires.

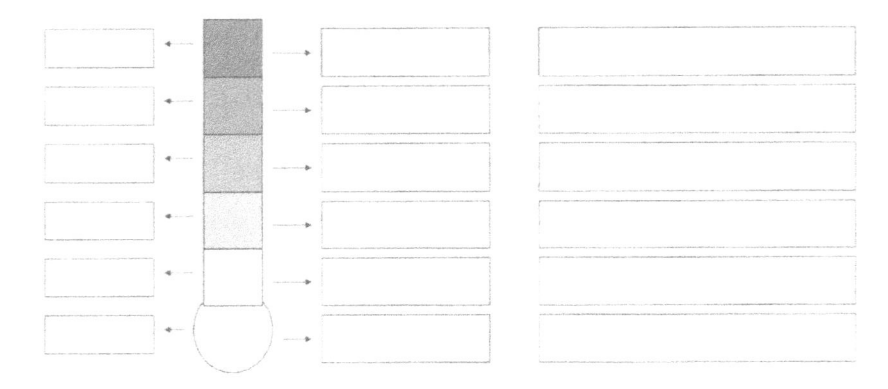

I had a choice between Word or Paint. It took me an entire morning to finish it, so don't be mean!

We started to work on it during our next session. We took the situations that made him angry and we put them in the corresponding column in order of intensity. The visual aid showing the colour gradients really helped him to put them in the order he had established. We'll look at the first column on the left next.

- *So, now it's time for the tricky part. You need to give a name to each of the states within the emotion, anger. This will help you to remember each one and to know whether or not it's very intense. How would you describe it when you're super angry?*
- *That's easy: rage!*

And that's what we wrote down. I should probably mention that Pedro, as is the case with lots of kids with Asperger's-type profiles, had an unusual verbal ability, which meant that this part of the task wasn't particularly complicated, but this isn't always the case.

We finished naming each emotion row, starting from the bottom with "upset" and ending up at the top with "rage".

> - *Now I get it – he said-, when something annoyed me, I expressed it powerfully, with so much intensity. But now I'm looking at it here, it's clearer that some things annoy me a little bit, but others annoy me so much more. I mean, if I compare them, I can see it.*

Pedro was right. Children on the spectrum live in the moment. In fact, they live everything intensely. They experience life with an intensity that us neurotypicals will rarely experience. But this can sometimes come at a cost, especially for them, as it can cause them significant suffering.

Now all that's left is to help express that emotion. At the time, I called it 'appropriate responses', not so much because it's appropriate for the surroundings, but for the person on the spectrum. This is where we can highlight emotional expressions (verbal and non-verbal communication, gestures, etc.) that accompany this intensity. Emotional communication is bilateral: if we use a type of body language the person with which we're communicating can understand, the communication is likely to be more effective. That's not to say that there's a sole (and valid) way to communicate emotions, not at all, but unfortunately, society has established expectations in this sense, as is the case in many other areas. Our job involves giving adequate tools to enable them to perform successfully, in all senses of the word. Ideally, whilst achieving greater awareness of diversity, we'll also demonstrate that their means of expressing emotions is valid, but such significant polarisation of these emotions can lead to consequences for the autistic person (as we've already seen) and the potential to be judged by those around them.

Careful though, not everything is dichotomic thinking, especially if we're working on a complex area, as is the case with emotions. In order to get a more comprehensive overview, we must mention alexithymia (R. Sivak, 1997) and mood swings. However, so as not to get too tied up with that here, we'll look at these concepts later on.

Alejandra Aceves "Alita" is a wonderful illustrator, author of a story and various books and is very active on Twitter (her username is @HistCotidianas, Historias Cotidianas), and she summarises all these concepts brilliantly in a cartoon she's given me permission to quote: "Do you know what happens to intense people like me? We're always full on. There's no peace and calm. We're like a whirlwind, a hurricane or a tornado… The glass is either dry, empty or overflowing and bubbling. Or joy is either immense or sadness unbearable".

Going back to polarised thinking, in adults the focus is on giving the autistic person a tool they can use when they see fit, but establishing from the get go that their way of thinking, perceiving and acting isn't necessarily wrong. Difficulties can arise when it comes to interacting with their surroundings. Sometimes it's very hard to ask the surroundings to adapt, and maybe making these adaptations ourselves can be valuable, as we can gain certain benefits from it. However, doing this continuously can be terrible. We'll talk about this towards the end of the book, in the chapter on autistic masking.

Is dichotomic or polarised thinking bad? Black or white thinking, as it's known in English. For Nick Dubin, autistic author of Asperger's Syndrome and Anxiety (2008): "Autistic people tend to judge events incorrectly". I don't fully agree with Nick. It's true that when it comes to socialising, autistic people face more challenges than their neurotypical peers. That's a fact, and it's partly due to polarised thinking, but there are other factors that I think are crucial, such as autistic hyperfocus, contrasted with central coherence (Attwood, 2006) and, in particular, autistic sequential processing compared to neurotypical parallel processing (as we saw in chapter 5). Is being very clear about your likes, dislikes and preferences such a bad thing? Isn't it just being self-aware? Is logic a bad thing? If you ask yourself this question, regardless of your condition you'll probably answer: "of course not".

This powerful sense of justice in autistic people could be explained by this firm, unchangeable psychological processing. Injustice by definition is an illogical situation or fact. Many people on the spectrum find it very difficult to process events that entail unjust and ultimately illogical consequences. Overheard in a conversation between a neurotypical person and an autistic adult:

- *This situation is unfair, that can't be.*
- *That's what the world is like. Sometimes unfair things happen and you can't do anything about it. You just have to accept it.*
- *I can't do that, it's incongruous, it's like accepting that I'm a different person. My mind can't process that.*

People on the spectrum tend to develop less friendships than their neurotypical peers, but they're incredibly rigid. For an autistic person, you're either their friend or you're not. There doesn't tend to be a mid-point or grey area. Let's go back to the question: is this way of thinking wrong? In theory, of course not, but in practice (and, in fact, it happens) this can give rise to many difficulties. What happens when a friendship doesn't correspond to an equal degree for both parties? This can lead to all types of problems, which tend to confuse and overwhelm the autistic person in particular. What happens if they consider the other person a friend, but, in reality they're just colleagues or peers from work or school?

The creation of these 'rigid categories in the autistic mind, these unchangeable realities (Klosko, et al. 2006), is a necessary part of their way of processing and perceiving information from their surroundings: it's their adaptive response to an incredibly changeable environment. The desire for invariance (Wing, 1982) becomes incredibly powerful from the moment in which the person on the spectrum begins to develop affective relationships that go beyond family. It's very common for an autistic child who has an argument with a friend to firmly state that "he's not my friend anymore, he's my enemy". As I always say, this, which is normally considered an immature form of expression and which isn't normally considered at the time, becomes an immature, exaggerated or inadaptive response when talking about an autistic adult. But in fact, it forms part of a very logical way of analysing reality, however, on the other hand, it can be the result of a non-erroneous analysis, as highlighted by Nick Dubin, but instead of a lack of information which can lead to a decision that the surroundings would likely deem "irrational".

With little ones (and not so little ones) we work on relationship circles: their versatility makes this one of the most useful tools to help people on the spectrum. It allows us to work on forming more specific thoughts as to where other people stand compared to us, depending on our relationship, what type of information they know and, consequently, how far we take a conversation topic (theory of mind) or what type of conversations are appropriate depending on the circle in which these people are situated. We can separate a 'friend' from a 'peer', as often these aren't synonyms, but they are sometimes. So, you're probably wondering, what does this depend on? There's no specific, right answer, the type the autistic mind needs, and for a hyper-logical mind (Peeters, 1994), that's the challenge. This series of concepts that neurotypical people process automatically and subconsciously is often an arduous task for someone on the spectrum who needs a clear, visual reference. Or, if this isn't the case, they can get lost in the maze that are social relationships.

STRANGERS, COMMUNITY SUPPORT, ACQUAINTANCES, FRIENDS, FAMILY.
Relationship circles. They're like a Swiss knife[48].

Sometimes people on the spectrum struggle to make friends. In therapy sessions I'm often asked, "When can we consider someone as a friend? What's the protocol? What steps to we

---

[48] A Swiss knife can have many uses, as is the case with this tool.

need to follow?". As I say, one of the biggest problems for people on the spectrum is that many of the areas in which they have difficulties don't come with a written manual of sorts. If we look back, from childhood, the majority of their difficulties are related to ambiguities, unwritten rules, lack of specificity and the 'grey area'. In these environments, dichotomous thinking can be a great ally (that great ally being hyperfocus[49]), but can become a challenge that is difficult to overcome. Many of the achievements of humankind have and will benefit from this innate ability to be clear on objectives and not give up because of the different voices that may say that this is not the right path to follow. This isn't usually the case in a mind that doubts, is ambiguous or changes its mind easily... neurotypical style.

As with almost all of the supposed symptoms associated with autism, dichotomous or polarised thinking is only an issue if you choose to see it that way. And, as with almost everything in life, although it can have a negative impact, it can also be positive.

Tips

Once the process of polarised thinking in autism has been described, we're going to see some practical examples of instances in which this way of thinking clashes when it comes to interaction with the neurotypical world.

---

[49] Hyperfocus or hyperconcentration is an intense form of mental concentration or visualisation focused on a limited topic, or beyond the objective reality and within subjective mental plans, concepts and imagination and other objects of the mind. Common in both autism and ADHD (attention deficit disorder and/or attention deficit hyperactivity disorder).

Non-autistic people, in general, talk for the sake of talking. In other words, they don't bear in mind the words they use or their true meaning. They can use very vehement phrases, such as 'that's the best' (referring to a videogame, for example) without having any intention to stick to that opinion. This can change in under a minute. The unpredictability of the surroundings taken to the personal extreme. Do they do this knowingly? The truth is, the answer is probably no in most cases. The typical response when you let them know that they've changed their opinion all of a sudden tends to be something along the lines of: "well, it's a way of speaking". So, why aren't you more precise? The answer is generally that neurotypical people don't have the need to be specific and can allow themselves that flexibility in the expressions they use.

People on the spectrum tend to look for precision both in terms of their environment and the people that surround them. Neurotypical people rarely speak with such precision, unless it's a very technical topic or something they're interested in, and even then, it isn't guaranteed.

As children, they tend to argue by using conversations such as:

- *My dad's the best.*
- *How do you know? Do you know all the dads?*
- *What do you mean? He just is.*
- *That's imprecise.*
- *What ever you say…*
- *Grrr…. You can't know that!*

Be specific or die!

Take a guess as to which child is autistic and which is neurotypical in this conversation.

This type of argumentation, one that isn't based on reality nor objective data, continues into adulthood, with slight changes. More than an objective data analysis that enables you to prove one thing or the other, the neurotypical person lets themselves be carried away by their emotions and makes a judgement, which may or may not have any value as regards objectives, but they can defend it as if their life depended on it, with no solid argument. For someone on the spectrum, you're either right or you're not. Black or white. And from this hyper-realistic perspective, their position is totally valid.

How many times has an autistic person not been involved in a group conversation because they haven't got enough information to give a valid argument? On the contrary, non-autistic people start to pass a judgment, even if they know nothing about the topic. Why? Are they not afraid of getting it wrong? Are they reckless? Many conversations are just trivial chatter, where any opinion goes: whether or not it's based on knowledge or not. Participation is what's important. However, the person on the spectrum tends to monitor their words closely, in order to be precise, but also out of fear of making a social error.

This tendency to be specific can sometimes lead to disregarding the adaptation of the surroundings (in other words, modifying our way of speaking in terms of form and content according to our listener) and, therefore, it can lead to a type of speech that can be considered out of place. The result: they take you for pedantic or a know-it-all. That rings a bell, right?

So, this adaptation is challenging for an autistic person. I remember that someone on the spectrum I used to work with said: "Why do I have to adapt my language to suit others? If they don't understand me, it's because their stupid and should learn". It could be that the speaker hasn't had the opportunity to learn language well, for example. You could miss out on the chance to communicate with someone for having prejudged them. Or perhaps you're talking to a child who doesn't understand you if you use very technical language, or with someone who is learning the language... Sometimes, not everything is black or white when referring to other people.

On the other hand, fear of making a social error tends to be taken to an extreme in autism. In general, the snowball effect, not acting quickly in the event of confusion when communicating, is much worse than the social 'error' itself, that can be rectified when asked about it later. A very clear example of this, and something that happens to lots of people on the spectrum, is putting off a question until formulating it even starts to cause anxiety or fear. Let's look at this situation: we're introduced to several people on our first day at work.

The combination of nerves, bad auditory memory and being focused on undertaking the technical task asked of us means we can barely remember anyone's name, or even nobody at all. The days go by, our work colleagues say hello to us, call us by our name, and we don't name them and use every single one of our cognitive resources to do everything possible to 'escape' these situations. Sooner or later, the others are going to realise that there's something going on. And they're going to judge us, no doubt: this is the snowball effect.

If we don't do anything, this distorted vision they have of us will increase. We need to act: it doesn't matter if it's been two days or two weeks. Not knowing what's really going on is always going to be the worst thing we can say to them. In general, the reaction of those around us tends to be very positive when we explain things. I've transcribed a conversation that tends to reoccur when we eventually find the courage to explain it:

- *I'm sorry, I'm really embarrassed to have to ask this: they told me your name on the first day, but I was so nervous and there were lots of people and I can't remember it. The days have gone by and I've just felt more and more embarrassed to ask you.*

- *Oh, don't worry! That's normal! I'm María. You're right, we should wear name badges on our shirts, shouldn't we?*

Although it doesn't appear so initially, these situations are also linked (among other processes, as we've seen and will see later on) with this polarised way of processing events, taking them to the extreme, even before we've got all the information. As I was saying, is processing this way a bad thing? Of course not. As we can see in the majority of situations where this can become an issue, it's due to interacting with an environment that processes differently.

We'll delve into analysing social interactions in chapter 12.

Chapter 8

Mood swings and alexithymia

"I'm like ammunition, I go from one emotional state to another almost violently (or at least that's what I've always been told). They always tell me to be calm, but I just can't. The truth is, I don't even know what that is". (Eva, 35 years old).

We can't talk about polarised thinking and its impact on emotional management in autistic people without talking about mood swings and alexithymia.

As we've seen in the previous chapter, autistic people tend to process things dichotomously, and this tends to be the case with emotions, too. So, how does this impact day-to-day life? We've spoken about specific situations, but the emotional flow is a daily occurrence in our lives. This leads us to ask the question, how does this occur in autism? As in many other instances, with a clinical term that assumes this way of processing is wrong, or at least not standard or adaptive. Not adaptive? For who? Well, for neurotypical people who process things differently. This is where the term mood swings comes into play[50]. When this instability is present together with behavioural alterations, agitation or irritability, it isn't unusual for some specialists to prescribe medications such as risperidone and aripiprazole[51].

In a few words, mood swings mean that autistic people can change mood incredibly quickly, sometimes going from one extreme to another. The label 'unjustifiably' is usually added here, as is 'incredibly quickly. But again, for who? It's true that mood swings can appear very confusing, even for some people on the spectrum, but generally speaking this is because these comparisons have been made with neurotypical people whose moods tend to last much longer and aren't usually so 'abrupt'.

When I try and explain the communication difficulties that occur between neurotypical parents or partners when one of them is autistic, I tend to use this image.

---

[50] Non-literal expression associated with scenic arts, meaning "to appear" or "show itself".
[51] Risperidone and aripiprazole are atypical antipsychotic medications commonly used in ASD and ADHD.

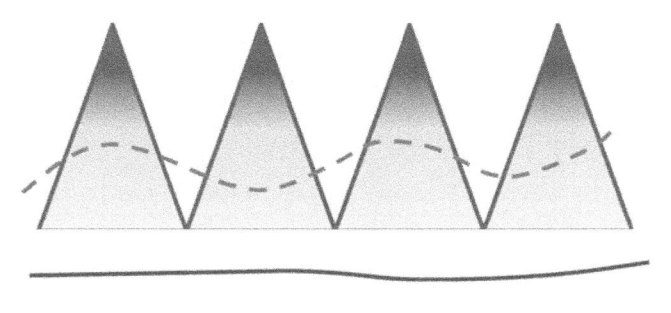

——— AUTISTIC POLARITY
- - - NEUROTYPICAL EMOTIONALITY

Emotional patterns in autism and neurotypical thinking: different in speed and intensity.

Many of the issues arise because autistic people and neurotypical people process emotions at different speeds and intensities. Generally speaking, autistic people experience this much more intensely, both positively and negatively, and go up and down more quickly. However, non-autistic people don't reach such polarised extremes and the speed this goes up and down is slower.

When there's a significant difference between both curves, the 'emotional distance' is so great that effective communication is very difficult. When a person on the spectrum is 'going down' (for example, something has happened and made them feel angry), the neurotypical person may still be taking it in or they haven't yet got rid of the feeling of anger. They're still in the 'descending curve' phase. As with everything else surrounding autism, all the processes we're talking about act together. For example, this is where an autistic person's logical thinking comes into play: as they're such practical people, they generally act sincerely and if they say 'I'm not angry anymore', that's the case. But it's actually quite common for a neurotypical person to say this, even if it appears otherwise (because it is). The classic autistic sincerity works against them once again, due to a false environment.

One of the people I diagnosed as autistic tended to have this sort of conversation with me:

-I mean, I get angry at my partner for something, we talk about it and everything is resolved. I do get really angry, actually.

- And how does he express it?

- Well, he doesn't appear to get angry, but this "not anger" hangs around for hours, or even days!

Another reason why there tends to be conflict between an autistic person and a neurotypical person is also linked to the different speeds of emotional expression. In general, an autistic person is more practical and pragmatic than someone who isn't on the spectrum, which can be explosive when trying to resolve a very emotionally charged situation.

Let's take the example of a non-autistic person who has just received bad news and is in shock. At that moment, the autistic person offers to help. What does the neurotypical person need at that time? In order to find out, we need to know where they are on the emotional curve. If they've just received the 'impact', they're still ascending slowly, as we've seen previously. Generally, at this time what they need is emotional support as opposed to solutions, which is what a pragmatic mind would offer, naturally. They wouldn't find it easy to put themselves in the other persons shoes[52] (see chapter on theory of mind). It isn't time to consider solutions until this curve starts to descend.

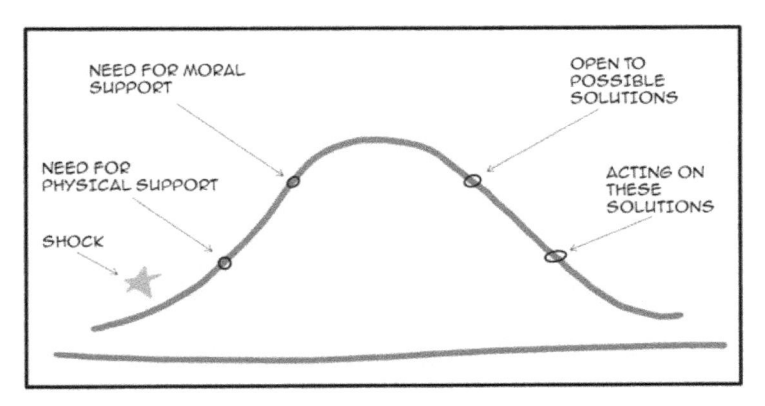

Neurotypical emotional processing: anything but practical.

Of course, this process doesn't only occur between autistic and neurotypical people, but in all types of people and relationships. In autism, however, pragmatism, logic, theory of mind and dichotomous thinking can be determining factors for (temporal/non-temporal) inadequacy of the possible consequential interaction. This is why it's crucial that we're aware of the different speeds of emotional regulation.

The following graph compares the ascent and descent of the emotional charge, and the moment when it is substituted by a more pragmatic thought charge, in addition to the overall differences between a person on the spectrum and a neurotypical person.

---

[52] Non-literal expression meaning to consider things from someone else's perspective.

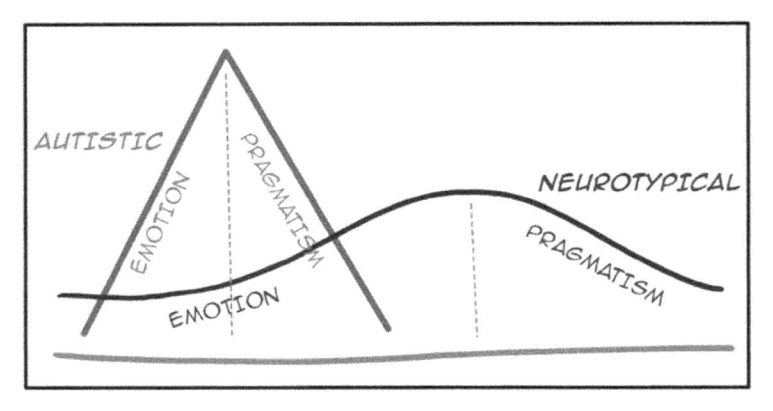

Speeds of autistic and neurotypical emotional processing.

At the end of the day, it's a question of speeds and timings that determines breakdowns in communication. Making a mutual effort to adapt these speeds and needs is a step in the right direction towards more effective communication.

Tips

In the previous chapter we were talking about the tendency to think dichotomously in autism, and how it led to a polarised emotional catharsis in terms of emotional expression. But what's emotional recognition like for people on the spectrum? In general, within the clinical field, it's said that autistic people have "difficulties identifying their own emotions and those of others"[53]. If we look at the sensory channel that gives us the most information – the visual channel – it appears that there's a tendency to omit certain signs (sometimes clear, sometimes subtle) on peoples' faces that would give the autistic person a significant amount of information regarding the emotional

---

[53] Different studies on visual processing of facial expressions in autism (Teunisse, 2003; Senju, 2004; Behmann, 2006).

state of those around them. Is that surprising? Not at all. Generally speaking, people on the spectrum find it hard to look at people's faces due to what it involves (as we've already seen in previous chapters); among other things, because there are too many information stimuli to focus on and process while the other person is speaking, which overwhelms them.

Many autistic children and adults have a history of abuse and forced facial positions so as to make them look at someone's face when they're speaking to them. In certain types of therapies, the autistic person is forced to adopt a communication posture that goes against their ability and way of processing information. This is all in order to make them 'pay attention', without taking into account that this act (which is an aversive technique: manually turning somebody's head), can cause them to becomes overwhelmed by stimuli and information that they are unable to collate. It comes as no surprise that the autistic community calls this 'conversion therapy'.

Even in the case of autistic people who do look at the speakers' face, the range of variable emotional expression is huge and, in general, with the exception of a few general keys, it's very difficult to be aware of all the possibilities without creating a prototype susceptible to change and variability, as required by the almost infinite possibilities (we'll talk about the creation of prototypes in the chapter on the symbolic field). In other words, it requires a sort of wild card that works for all types of expressions (from the most explicit to the most subtle) and, in general, autistic processing occurs completely differently, as we've seen in chapter 5. In addition, the fact that the emotional expression doesn't always correspond to what the person we're talking to is saying (not to mention the information we can gain from the rest of their non-verbal communication), is an added challenge. This is where most recognition difficulties occur in autism: various information channels to process in parallel, in addition to comparing the information, which instead of providing similarities sometimes results incongruous. The result: total confusion, in addition to the feeling of 'deceit' the autistic person.

So, what should we do? María says: "I'm tired of asking something everyone else deems obvious. They say, can't you see it in my face? Actually no, I can't. So, I end up not saying anything and get a surprise every now and again". María has hit the nail on the head[54]: when we're talking about children, we can offer certain strategies, such as asking questions if we're unsure of how somebody else is feeling, but when we get to a certain age, people assume that everyone has certain knowledge and skills.

Trying to undertake this parallel processing, with the addition of a stimulus that causes you significant stress, goes against your very nature as an autistic person. In certain situations where we feel safer, such as at home, we can ask speakers to try and be more coherent with the information they're communicating to us, and to even give us feedback on our interpretation (please do this in an uncondescending way). In other cases, such as at work, we should probably be more cautious and use other, less direct strategies in order to confirm this information. Work contexts tend to give rise to many confusing situations, being one of the contexts within which one would least expect such variability, given the nature of the more formal or professional role that people should supposedly take on (and where there should be more coherent and unequivocal emotional information). Perhaps this is why peo-

---

[54] Non-literal expression meaning to have found the answer.

ple on the spectrum are most likely to be faced with frustrating situations.

This difficulty when it comes to recognising emotions is indeed a hindrance, but only when the autistic person communicates with a neurotypical person (Crompton, 2019). When autistic people communicate with each other, they don't have issues with this recognition: whether that be because they give more importance to the message being communicated, or because their expressions and the message correspond (there's no incongruence between the emotion communication channels). However, clinical literature on autism studies maintains that a deficit in emotional recognition is key to understanding the difficulties faced by people on the spectrum when it comes to socialising. Again, if we look at this through the prism of neurotypical processing, it's logical that autistic processing appears to have significant consequences when it comes to socialising. What if we try to use their processing style and, as neurotypical people, adapt to it? What if we provide tools to strengthen their skills instead of requiring them to use those that are adapted to us?

In terms of recognising their own emotions, it's common to come across autistic people who, when asked "how do you feel?", answer "I don't know". I can't even imagine how many times parents or teachers of autistic children have become angry because the child "can't be bothered to respond" or say something along the lines of "are you having me on? What do you mean you don't know how you are?".

This can be explained by two phenomena. The first is dichotomous thinking which, as we've seen, causes autistic people to express themselves intensely in terms of emotional extremes and, yet, to find themselves in emotional limbo at the same time when they can't locate themselves at either extreme. The second is the phenomena known as alexithymia.

In some questionable publications, given the limited sample used in their studies, tend to associate alexithymia in autism as a characteristic in itself, insofar as the person on the spectrum being more likely to experience anxiety and depression than the neurotypical population (which is true), and that in these moments when alexithymia appears (which is completely incorrect).

In autism, alexithymia is understood as difficulty recognising one's own emotions, and occurs throughout the person's life and at all times. However, its impact varies greatly between people on the spectrum, which is why it's not currently considered a diagnostic criterion.

As explained by Mahler (2015), internal perception mechanisms (or interoception, as she calls them), partly lead to alexithymia in autism, which we'll look into further in chapter 11. Just as in autism there can be difficulties in terms of perceiving different internal stimuli such as hunger or thirst, challenges are also faced when it comes to perceiving and processing internal signs that give us information regarding the processes that regulate, and thus define, our emotions.

How can we explain dichotomous thinking in terms of its relationship to alexithymia? If we think back to black or white thinking, it's hard to fit this thought construct into the breadth of the description of emotions. So, what can we do? As I always say: the first rule of autism is to use visual aids. These types of diagrams can help our mind better locate itself within the frame of emotional recognition, by going from a more global (more general) category to a more specific one.

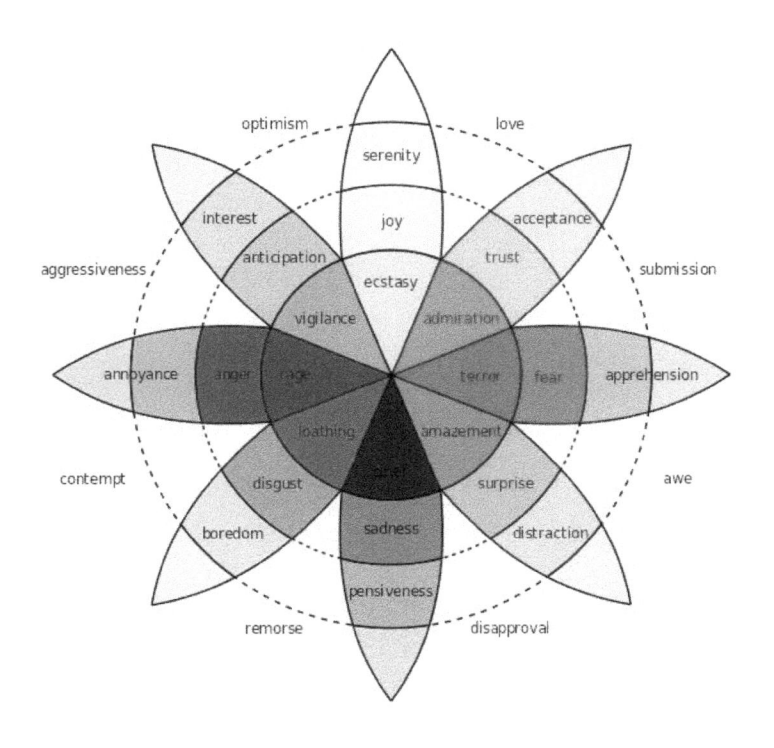

Plutchick's Wheel of Emotions.

If we're working with or trying to help children, we'll need to simplify this scale and gradually make it more complex. It's important to show physical or bodily sensations to help them recognise them and take note of them on the scales we make, so that they've always got them to hand. It's particularly important to show them that there are no negative or positive emotions (which is sometimes difficult to understand from a dichotomous perspective), just different intensities.

"If you're sad, why don't you have a sad face? Is feeling sad a bad thing?" (Miguel, 10 years old).

Chapter 9

Empathy and theory of mind

"My husband says I'm too blunt and I hurt his feelings, but that's never my intention" (Marta, 36 years old).

If there's one myth the autistic community has spent years trying to debunk, it's the supposed lack of empathy in people on the spectrum. Interestingly, hyper empathy is becoming increasingly associated with autistic people, which is just a never-ending paradox.

Below, I'll give a very personal example I shared with CE-PAMA (an organisation that works with women and girls on the spectrum) in the April 2020 edition of their magazine, which focused on the concept of empathy. I'll use this as a starting point to begin to clear up all these concepts.

> My mother passed away recently. During that incredibly painful time, besides my family, the friend who I felt closest to and who truly supported me and was the most concerned about me during and after the process, is autistic. I could see the genuine concern for me in her face, the look in her eyes and her gestures. Her tears weren't a result of emotional contagion (I'll

talk about that later actually), or a social mask. It was pure, raw empathy.

I have to admit that at times my friend doesn't realise when her listener is tired of the conversation, or perhaps doesn't give the required information when telling a story. But that doesn't mean to say she doesn't feel or connect emotionally with other people. In fact, it's likely her more logical way of perceiving the world makes her more sensitive than any neurotypical person, as much of a paradox as that seems. Because when she feels something, she truly feels it, with no half measures or masks.

I'm not falling for the bad translations that exist surrounding theory of mind. There are no excuses. If you're intent on saying that an autistic person has no empathy, that's to say you haven't spent more than two minutes with someone on the spectrum. Get out of your office. Stop looking at books written by prominent psychiatrists, psychologists and neurologists, and go and experience their reality.

It'll enrich your world, just as it did mine.

With such a clear, evident example of empathy, why is there such a widespread belief that autistic people lack empathy? I mentioned some of the key aspects in this small text I wrote for the CEPAMA magazine.

Theory of Mind (ToM) is one of the most relevant theories in autism. In fact, it's one of the key differentiating factors when undertaking a differential diagnosis. Where other characteristics are commonly associated with autism, they're not exclusive to this condition (as we've seen in chapter 4), conversely, the concept of theory of mind, when understood correctly of course, is a characteristic almost exclusive to people on the spectrum.

But the concept of theory of mind itself isn't exclusive to autism. It's actually an expression that originates from anthropological theories (Bateson, 1982) and other fields of psychology (Premack, Woodruff, 1978) and even philosophy, and therefore information regarding ToM isn't always directly related to autism. This is potentially why there's such widespread confusion regarding the concepts addressed by this theory as regards their application to autism.

No, that's not what I mean.

Going back to basics, just so we're on the same wavelength[55], the mechanism of theory of mind "is a system that allows us to infer the full range of emotional states based on behaviour. In other words, to establish a theory of mind" (Baron-Cohen, 1995). It's something similar to having this 'intuitive psychology' (yes, intuition as opposed to certainty) regarding other people based on the observation of their behaviour, whether they're very evident or perhaps very subtle.

According to Baron-Cohen (1999), people on the spectrum encounter variable difficulty when it comes to these inferences according to their observations of other people. As regards subtle behaviours, this difficulty is increased due to the greater quantity of information being either fragmented, multichannel (parallel processing), or often depending on the emotional interpretation of facial expressions and other mechanisms of non-verbal communication.

Consequently, the person on the spectrum may experience the following, among others:

- Difficulty considering what the other person may know about a specific topic and, consequently, not giving the necessary elements in a conversation.

- Difficulty detecting when the listener loses interest in the conversation.

- Difficulty understanding the figurative sense of the speaker's message.

---

[55] Non-literal expression meaning that we all have the same understanding.

- Difficulty understanding unwritten social rules or norms.

- Difficulty understanding other people's moods.

Here we can observe some of the difficulties encountered when trying to find a global theory that, by way of one sole principle, explains the full reality of autism. The truth is, it's impossible. As I mentioned in the introduction, the reality of the autistic condition is so rich and complex that the only real way of explaining it is continuously combining all the processes that act complementarily to each other. ToM cannot be studied without taking into account executive functions (Ozonoff et al., 1991), central coherence (Happé, 2000) or, what I consider to be even more relevant, symbolic capacity and sequential processing.

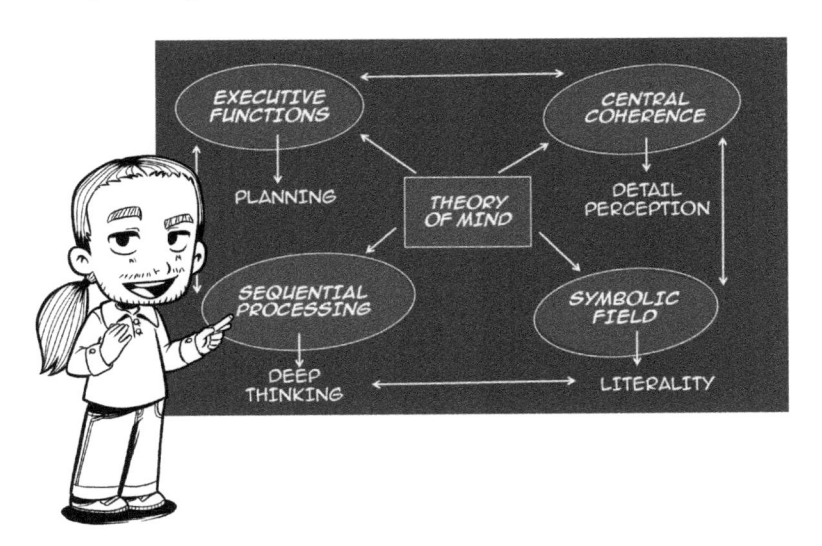

Theory of mind and its relation to other processes in autism.

Often, when talking to autistic children, we come to realise that they may not be taking into account what the other person might know when, for example, they tell us about a film. In this case, to which initially we wouldn't give much consideration due to their age, can actually be a very significant hindrance as the person grows and develops less tolerant of errors. In the text I shared with CEPAMA, the one at the beginning of the chapter, I gave the example of my friend Marina, who's autistic.

When Marina and I talk about work-related things, for example, she sometimes tells me certain things I'm not aware of or maybe even talks to me about people I don't know or whom she's never mentioned in previous conversations. She doesn't introduce those details, as she doesn't stop to think whether or not I know them. She automatically just assumes. So, she basically talks as though all the content of her thought processes regarding that specific topic was present in my own mind.

Let's take a look at another example. Carlos, a 12-year-old autistic boy, wants to ask his mum for a favour. When he gets home, he sees that she's in the kitchen, and without even saying hello, he asks:

- *Mum, can I have money to buy some cards?*

His mum replies:

- *Can't you see this isn't a good time?*

Besides the fact that she replied with a rhetorical question (ultra-metarepresentation, see chapter 10 later on), which confuses Pablo even more, the key here is that Pablo hasn't considered the potential negative impact of this on his mum based on her mood. At the time, his mum had just come off the phone and was irritated by a conversation she had just had. Had Pablo used ToM, he would probably have understood that it wasn't a good time to ask, anticipating the negative response him mother might give him because of her mood.

Let's take a look at some more examples: Pablo again, who loves volcanoes, has lots of friends at school and often brings up his conversation topic so that he can tell them everything he knows about volcanoes. His friends appear to be fed up of it already, and they tend to say: "Pablo, stop it, you're too full on". Pablo doesn't understand why his peers don't like volcanoes as much as he does. He doesn't know how to get involved.

This situation occurs throughout the autism spectrum. The issue, among many others, is what happens when the person and their surroundings start to grow up. Rejection from others in response to him trying to interact with them becomes increasingly more subtle and, therefore, difficult to detect as an autistic person, who they end up leaving out, with no clear explanation.

This mind-blindness (Baron-Cohen, 1995) means the person on the spectrum has more difficulties when it comes to predicting the behaviour of others, such as intentions or desires. This would explain why many autistic people are often caught out by the actions of others.

The fact that they're unaware of the social cues that help to start and maintain conversations can be partially explained by theory of mind: a prior analysis must be undertaken prior to these inferences in order to know how to act (for example, in order to know if a person is busy at the time or is able to speak to us). There's no written protocol for each and every social situation, as people on the spectrum tend to request, but there are certain general key points that can later be adapted to different situations. However, that would imply flexibility and generalisation, both of which are aspects that autistic people find very difficult.

Of course, an autistic person's hyper-logical thinking could argue that as neurotypicals who use theory of mind, we're only making predictions based on assumption, as opposed to pragmatic or objective reality. And they'd be completely right. The fact is that the foundations of certain social relationships are often based on these interpretations that are made constantly. In social relationships, people don't wait until they've got all the information before acting, which is why they act based on these assessments, these inferences that may be right or wrong. Someone on the spectrum generally prefers to receive information first-hand:

"I don't know when it's a good time to talk to my partner. I always tell them that. I'd rather they told me straight than have to guess if they're ok or not, or if they're able to talk". (José, 38 years old)

The assessment of skills as regards theory of mind is one of the biggest challenges during a neuropsychological assessment, for the reasons we'll see later on. In general, when it comes to assessing children we use the Sally-Anne test, designed by Baron-Cohen in 1995.

The Sally-Anne test consists of putting the child on the spectrum in a situation in which they have to observe the actions of two girls who have a basket, a box and a ball. Ideally this will be done in 3D, with figures or dolls, as opposed to just a 2D image which, on the other hand, can be subject to symbolic interpretation[56]. The following image shows the action exactly as it appears.

---

[56] Some research such as that undertaken by Leslie and Frith in 1988 attributed the fault to the symbolic field as opposed to ToM, as it was represented on paper.

Updated version of the Sally and Anne task.

The child is then asked: Where will Sally look for her marble? If they use ToM, they'll reply with Sally's knowledge, which is that she's going to look for it in her basket because she (Sally) hasn't seen Anne take her marble and put it in her box. In other words, they'll put themselves in Sally's mind to respond based on what Sally knows, instead of responding with all the information they've got in their power.

But classic first order or second order theory of mind tests only detect very flagrant cases of these empathy difficulties (Baron-Cohen et al., 1997). Generally speaking, all neurotypical children 'pass' this test from 4 years old onwards in first order, and from 5 or 6 years old in more complex, second order cases.

So, what do we do? The rich nature of autism and its variability (ultimately, its spectrum), constitute tremendous difficulty in terms of undertaking standardised tests that can be applied throughout the variability of this condition (Baron-Cohen, Leslie and Frith, 1985). At the end of the day, the best thing to do is to analyse the person in real life, far from their performance in a controlled and artificial situation. Only then will we have an idea of the magnitude of the impact of ToM on each person.

Does this mean that autistic people are unable to undertake this process at cognitive level? Not at all. The fact that this is a very mechanical way of learning and it poses significant energy consumption for the person on the spectrum, given that they have to undergo a process for which their brain is simply just not designed, as we saw in chapter 5. As we'll see later on, the challenge is that this process requires planning and parallel processing, and this has to be done very quickly. And sometimes you have to throw all logical reasoning out the window![57]

In my case, I tend to use lots of role-playing games to strengthen this ability in adolescents and young people. In a role-playing game, each participant plays a character with a series of physical and mental characteristics and, therefore, the player should react to what happens to their character based on these characteristics, not their own. Also, often one of the plays receives information that the other players must ignore, as their character doesn't know it and they must therefore act accordingly. Theory of mind, plain and simple.

- *When my peers are distracted, I grab all the gold and escape at night.*
- *What are you doing? We're friends!*
- *My character and your character aren't friends. In fact, he's a thief.*
- *But, but…*

Going back to real life, according to a study published by the American Psychiatric Association (2016), the main problem for people on the spectrum are inadequate responses: "The lack of social skills for autistic people and their limited experience regarding relationships leads them to respond in an unexpected way. Sometimes they don't know how to act". As you'll have guessed, I don't agree with this statement at all. Even though it's true that this is often the consequence, I think that other factors intervene when it comes to responding:

1) When there's inaction or, in other words, the autistic person doesn't respond at all, this tends to be due to a

---

[57] Non-literal expression that means to discard a certain belief, concept or theory.

history of failing when it comes to offering their alternative. Also, other factors may come into play here. Let's take the example of hugging someone who has received some sudden, bad news and bursts into tears:

A) The person on the spectrum may have tactile sensitivity and consequently find hugging difficult.

B) They might not be sure of how to give a hug, nor its duration or intensity. An autistic person doesn't tend to improvise and they need all the information.

2) The autistic person may give a response that although not inappropriate, nor is it what the other person was expecting. For example, looking for a solution to the problem that is affecting the person who is upset.

So, is this a lack of social skills? It's more like a lack of adaptation to their emotional state to suit that of the other person, due to many factors, in particular the different speed of emotional patterns, as we saw in chapter 8. I'm convinced that, if the person who demands the hug were to offer all the information necessary regarding their needs as opposed to just insinuating in order for the autistic people to work it out, things would be very different.

"I love my partner a lot, but sometimes the situation is too much for me. Everything is so fast and I feel overwhelmed. This means I end up paralysed and I don't know how to respond. But if they were to tell me what they need at that time, I'd do it, even if I think it's impractical. I know we go at different speeds" (Alicia, 40 years old).

On the other hand, if we think of the fact that autistic people process things in a way that's very real, vivid and intense, partly due to dichotomic or polarised thinking, it comes as no surprise that they encounter situations with overwhelming emotional contagion. This is sometimes truly surprising in children: situations where parents are upset and their child suddenly runs over to give them a hug or cry with them. I'm often asked: "If a child is unable to empathise, where does this behaviour come from?".

The answer is that they're two different processes. Emotional contagion occurs due to stimulatory overwhelm towards one of the emotional extremes (for example, in a case of happiness or euphoria, the child may react by jumping for joy), which cause this contagion due to assimilation or emotional recognition (we talk about this in the chapter on dichotomous thinking). In the adequate empathetic response, the one people expect, the autistic person has to use theory of mind to gauge the mental (information) and emotional (feelings) state of the others involved, in order to then act. This is a much more complex process that includes parallel processing and, occasionally, the demand requires this to be done extremely quickly.

Now we understand the concept of emotional contagion, and if we also add processing and sensory sensitivity into the mix, it's no surprise that autism becomes increasingly linked to hyper empathy. In this case, the concept is sometimes associated with the processing of external stimuli, although on other occasions this is more in line with the concept of empathy associated with the theory of mind we've been talking about in this chapter. This is the case according to psychiatrist Sandra L. Brown who, in her book *Women who love psychopaths* (2008), explains the behaviour and justification of women who are emotionally tied to psychopaths using the concept of hyper empathy.

On the other hand, and no need for fine-tuning, this concept could fit in perfectly within the theoretical paradigm of the intense world (Markram, 2007). According to this neuropsychologist:

> Let's propose that the autistic person can perceive their surroundings not only as overwhelming […] the autistic person can try to face the intense and aversive world through avoidance. Therefore, deteriorated social interactions and distancing cannot be the result of a lack of compassion, inability to put themselves in the position or lack of emotivity of the other person, but instead, the complete opposite occurs as a result of an environment perceived intensely, if not painfully.

We'll talk about perception and sensitivity in autism later on, in chapter 11.

Tips

Theoretical constructs aside, the important part is that once the implications of theory of mind in social relationships are understood, or at least how they're understood by neurotypicals, is what do we do if we're on the spectrum?

As I've been explaining throughout this book, I don't see the way people on the spectrum perceive the world and consequently, engage with it, as erroneous. If anything, it's the opposite: it's a logical, ordered perception based on information and pragmatism. But it's without a doubt that the impact of social pressure makes having some tools to use, when there's no alternative, inevitable.

As we've seen in this chapter, neurotypical people use ToM for anticipation and modulate their behaviour based on inference of the emotional states and thoughts of others. This doesn't mean to say that the information is 100% true, nor, of course, that this information is used correctly (we'll talk about lies in the chapter on social relationships).

By undertaking fast, parallel processing, they adapt their behaviour based on those prototypes of social behaviour created and that can be modified according to the circumstances and different contexts. These are things that people on the spectrum can do by creating written protocols of action, even if it's more mechanical. A very important part in terms of the creation of these protocols is to be clear that they're not 'closed systems' and that, therefore, they're susceptible to changes. Thanks to these changes, we can create a series of actions for different contexts.

An autistic person might find it difficult to perceive the other person's emotional state, especially if the signs are very subtle. A good strategy is to always ask how the other person is and if it's a good time to talk to them.

One of the clearest situations where ToM can trick us is during conversations, especially informal ones (where there are less protocols, making them more unpredictable). In order to solve these issues and ensure a successful interaction, we need to keep the following in mind:

1) We should know what the other person knows about the conversation topic. If we don't have this information, we can ask. This way, we can add in more or less elements. Starting a conversation about autism with someone with previous knowledge isn't the same as talking to someone who completely overlooks the topic. The best strategy is to always ask.

- *Hi. What do you know about autism?*
- *Well, I'm an occupational therapist and I work in the field of autism.*

2) In light of the foregoing, we should adapt what we're going to say according to what they know about the topic. We shouldn't include unnecessary explanations.

For example, adding this into a conversation might not be the right thing to do:

- *Well, as you already know, Leo Kanner described autism in 1943...*
- *Yeah, I already know who Leo Kanner is...*

3) We should ask for feedback every so often. As it's complicated to be paying attention to someone's non-verbal communication while we're talking, it's possible that by not doing this, we don't realise that maybe the conversation is boring them. It's also important we ask our listener for their opinion.

- *Do you want me to carry on? Am I boring you?*
- *No, don't worry, it's interesting.*

4) It's important to add in parts of their discourse into our own. This way, we give them feedback and they'll know that we're keeping them in mind, even if we don't agree with what they've said.

- *Well, actually there were other authors who described autism before Kanner...*

- *Yes, you're right. Sukhareva, for example. But as I was saying...*

This is an error that although more common in children, it also occurs in some autistic adults. It's one of the things with perhaps the most consequences, as neurotypical people may even see it as very disrespectful.

Of course, in more familiar environments, the person on the spectrum should rest, be able to be themselves and not have to use these strategies. This is when 100% of adaptations are to be made by the people around them (close relationships). We'll talk about this later on, in chapter 12.

With children, visual aids are key in helping to give them some tools to enable them to resolve these situations. Problems tend to arise due to a lack of tact and inadequate social behaviours.

Often, their models of interaction are based on TV programmes or cartoons, where they use blunt and surprising expressions. But ultimately, the lack of these mentalist anticipation skills leads to them being considered disrespectful, blunt, selfish and inadequate, at the very least.

We often hear people say that autistic children 'don't have a filter'. They say the first thing that pops into their mind, without thinking about the potential consequences. The truth is, what happens is that this inference that ordinarily occurs in ToM doesn't happen, they don't anticipate the impact that what they say may have on other people. Of course, other concepts such as hyperrealism play a key role in these situations:

- *Pablo, you can't call me old.*
- *But you are old, you're older than me.*

- *But if you call me old, you're insulting me.*
- *So, when we say that the kitchen table is old, we're insulting it?*

To resolve this situation, Pablo should 'theorise' that his mother might feel hurt if he calls her old, as this is a construct that could be offensive in certain circumstances and social contexts. Arrgh, it's so complicated once we analyse it, isn't it? It really is, and much more so that it may initially appear. This is why incredibly frustrating situations occur for parents, and especially in children.

We should help them by using visual strategies and always offer them communication alternatives. It's important we show them the mechanisms that regulate conversations, because it's common for a lad on the spectrum to go up to a peer or an adult, goes on and on and then walks off. At first, they don't let him know what has gone wrong with that interaction style, but people gradually become aware that something 'isn't working' and the worst part is that they don't know what it could be.

We'll talk about all this in more depth in chapter 12.

Chapter 10

Symbolic understanding

"Today my mum said: you can be in mass and misbehaving at the same time. I didn't understand a bloody word she said" (Autistic adult).

"Daniel, explain this joke to me:
"Jaimito, if you're really upset, what should you do?"
"Cry me a river"
"That doesn't make any sense, I couldn't possibly cry an entire river, I'd run out of tears. Nobody can do that" (Javier, 19 years old).

Perhaps the least understood concept when it comes to understanding the world of autism is the symbolic field. In general, this concept is reduced to that of 'symbolic play' and, therefore, its impact is normally explored in terms of autistic children, totally overlooking this cognitive process in adults.

But it's hardly our fault, is it? Publications about autism and diagnostic screening questionnaires, as well as the professionals themselves, really give significant importance to whether the child engages in imaginative play or not, if they invent characters or create stories, or if, on the other hand, they just line objects up or spin their toy car wheels around, without driving them around on the floor.

The reality is, this concept is much broader and, as we'll see later on, it's perhaps the most important field in terms of understanding the reality of autism, its characteristic way of perceiving reality and the explanation for many people of the hidden aspects surrounding this condition. From the false declarations that say that autistic people have no imagination, to the explanation as to why some children struggle with language.

Symbolic ability is that which enables us to imagine and create other realities. Some of these can be created from nothing, but generally, existing realities are taken, transformed and recreated to give new realities, which may be more or less original or similar or different to the starting reality. Even just understanding this concept we can already see that it goes beyond the ability to play (symbolically).

We're going to work with a graphic concept to help understand this topic. It may appear very complex, but it's actually quite simple (but it does have huge implications).

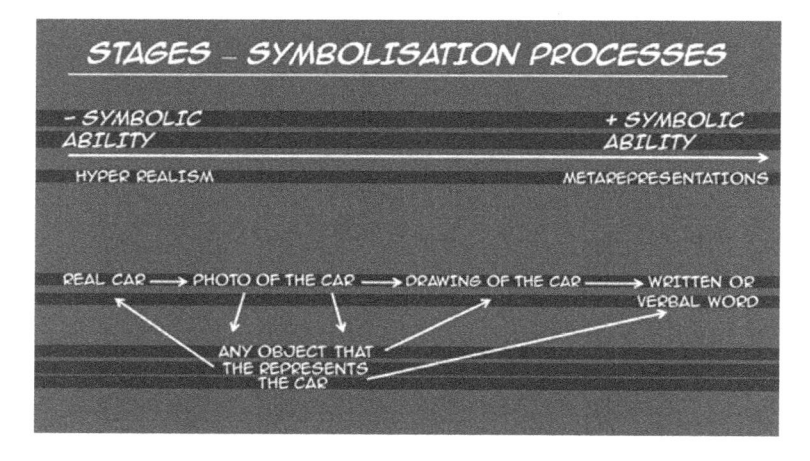

The symbolisation process.

In this example, we're going to take the idea of a car. Symbolic ability is the ability to create metarepresentations (a concept taken from linguistics), which are constructs that refer to that specific reality; in this case, the real element is the car. Any substitution of the car is a metarepresentation, and each one implies a suspension of reality. In other words, the photo of the car isn't the actual car, but a (symbolic) representation of it. It we want to complicate this further; we'll substitute the photo for a drawing of the car. The drawing of the car is a representation of the photo (which at the same time represents the real car), therefore, it's a double negation of reality. And it we represent it with the written word "car", it makes things even more complicated because there's no visual reference point (basically, the word car doesn't look anything like a real car).

If we look at it from the perspective of a hyperrealistic perception as described by Theo Peeters (2008) to people on the spectrum, it only makes sense: what does the word 'cat' have in common with a real cat? Nothing. In fact, in any case, the onomatopoeia 'meow' is more like the real thing, isn't it? At least the sound is similar. But 'cat'? It's nothing but a very, very complex representation of a specific reality.

Are all people on the spectrum able to create these metarepresentations? In theory, yes. What often happens (which is why a previous assessment of this area is crucial) is that we expect the person to make an effort for which they may not be prepared. One of the keys in autism is errorless learning[58]. It must be done this way, because otherwise, if we subject an autistic per-

---

[58] Errorless learning refers to a form of training which tries to avoid the person who is beginning to learn a certain type of information making mistakes, the opposite to traditional education where errors form part of the learning process itself.

son to exert themselves above and beyond their cognitive possibilities at this point in development, we may provoke total rejection and a feeling of frustration and failure, which is sometimes difficult to revert.

It's important to start small and work our way up: start with the most real and least metaphorical system (real objects) and slowly start complicating things using the framework I've shown above. The idea is to get to the last metarepresentation step: written language (much more important than spoken language, as it still remains over time). This is a basic, not only for communication interventions, but also for all the anticipation systems. All of these should be adapted to the symbolic level of the autistic person in question.

This is why in autism, the fact that a child plays with a pencil imagining it's a car or plane is a good indicator: they're creating metarepresentations that are key in terms of accessing language.

So, where do Asperger's syndrome profiles fit into this explanation? Well, in the last twist in terms of language, which is its 'artistic' use. This is what I call ultra-metarepresentation.

Let's take the example of the written word 'cat', and dissect[59] it from the least to the most symbolic use.

The minimum level of symbolisation is zero symbolisation. So, we're referring to the real cat. The next one could be a 3D replica of this cat, but life-size. If we change the size, we get to a larger degree of symbolisation (we must also remember the need to adapt to reality and not take kindly to change). We continue and move on to a photo. In this case, we leave be-

---

[59] In this context, dissect means to examine or to study.

hind the three dimensional one and move onto a 'flat' representation of the cat. It must be the same cat (we'll talk about the creation of prototypes later on), not just any cat. If we use just any cat, in terms of symbolisation we would be at the next level: drawing. This is the pictorial representation of reality, which gives rise to a plethora of possibilities (and difficulties), as it very much depends on the type of pictorial representation. In principle, a representation that's as close to reality as possible could help to establish the symbolic relationship between the real cat and the drawing, but sometimes a more simple but clearer and universal, can be easier (especially if what we're trying to do is create a universal prototype, which we'll see later on). The next level of complexity, or symbolisation, would be the representation of the cat with the written word 'cat', which, as we mentioned earlier, doesn't look anything like the real thing, nor does it sound the same. In general, when learning, both are presented together so that the person on the spectrum associates both representations.

Is that the end? Not at all. Humans, or rather, neurotypicals, have a strange habit of complicating language. A person on the spectrum once said to me: "You neurotypicals all think you're poets. Why don't you just say what you want, without all the bells and whistles?[60]. And they were right.

- *I'm from Valencia. Where are you from?*
- *I'm a cat.*
- *But, but…*

---

[60] Non-literal expression that refers to unnecessary information or extras that do not add any meaning.

[Comic panels: Boy on phone saying "I'M FROM VALENCIA." / "I'M A CAT." Other boy reacts "WHAT?" then sees a cat on phone saying "MEOW!"]

It's finally happening.

Is the speaker saying that they're not a human, but a cat? Maybe someone born in Madrid knows the meaning of this expression, with its origins in the Middle Ages. I'm not going to go into it here, but in short, someone whose both parents were born in Madrid can be called *gato* or cat.

In Asperger-type profiles, these difficulties in terms of symbolic abilities are represented in the following twist on metarepresentations, such as double entendre, set phrases or non-literal language: ultra-metarepresentations. Again, these are forms of negating reality: we want to say one thing, but what we say (or write) is another.

"Look at what Bon Jovi sings here; he's exaggerating. He says that to show his love for his partner he would climb the world's highest mountain. That's Everest, which has an altitude of 8849 metres. That's dangerous. Even if you're accompanied by the most skilled locals, there's no guarantee you'll make it and survive. It's absurd, because he lives in the USA. In the time it takes him to go to the Himalayas and back, I bet his girlfriend isn't still waiting for him…" (Martín, 14 years old, autistic)

Metarepresentations are used continuously in both spoken and written language. And that's without even going into poetry (or song, as we've seen), where they're used almost continuously. Whether more or less so, all types of language disciplines use this language resource.

> **Crautista**
> @crautista
>
> #Literalidad
> Hoy en clase de literatura he tenido que explicar qué significaba "y la puerta del taxi se la llevó para siempre" Y yo solo podía imaginarme una puerta con forma humana que se llevaba a la mujer muy lejos 😩

Tweet by @crautista[61]. For people on the spectrum, it's often impossible to avoid creating this literal image in their mind.

What are these ultra-metarepresentations? We can classify them in a series of groups, as we can see in the following table.

---

[61] #Literal. In today's literature class I had to explain what "and the taxi door took her away and she was never seen again" meant. I just imagined a door in the shape of a human taking the woman really far away!

ULTRA-METAREPRESENTATIONS			
RHETORICAL FIGURES	LITERARY FIGURES	LANGUAGE RESOURCES	CULTURAL EXPRESSIONS
- METAPHORS - SIMILES	DOUBLE ENTENDRE	- IRONY - SARCASM - NON-SPECIFICS	- SAYINGS - SET PHRASES - SLANG

Outline of the ultra-metarepresentations.

Describing each of them:

- Metaphors: in a metaphor, a reality or concept is expressed using a reality that although different, is linked in some way.

"You're in your prime" (prime is understood as youth and height of life).

- Similes: a simile consists of establishing similarities or comparison between two images, ideas, feelings, things, etc. Unlike the metaphor, it tends to include a word as a comparative nexus (like, equal to, as).

"Your eyes are like two twinkling stars" (it means your eyes are bright and sparkling).

- Phrases with double entendre: this is when a sentence could be understood in one of two ways. Jokes tend to be based on this. When taken to the extreme, this would be absurd humour, which looks for the limits of reality. This type of humour, just like in literal jokes, tends to be more enjoyable for people on the spectrum than other plays on words.

"Your head is in the clouds" (to be distracted). "It's right under your nose" (what you're looking for is right in front of you, but you can't see it).

- Irony: irony often involves body language and intonation, which form part of the discourse, given that this demonstrates that what is actually being said isn't actually referring to that, but actually to something else.

"Aren't you fed up of studying?" (said to a child who, instead of studying as we'd expect, is actually playing, for example).

Rhetorical questions are also part of this category.

"Who do you think you're talking to?" (this question actually expresses the other person's non-conformity with your way of speaking or meaning behind your message).

- Sarcasm: sarcasm is the use of irony as a resource to offend or insult someone else, or at least, "make them realise".

"Thanks. If you hadn't have told me, I wouldn't have noticed" (expresses how tedious it is when you already realised something, but they draw attention to it as if you were unaware).

- Sayings and set phrases: a saying or set phrases is a phrase or expression that has a set form and a figurative meaning. These are commonly used by the majority of speakers belonging to a linguistic community.

"Like father, like son" (meaning they are incredibly alike).

"Get stuffed!" (meaning *"leave me alone"*)

- Slang: a group of expressions used in a particular cultural or geographic context. Sometimes associated with a type of profession or role.

  "Give us a smoke" (give me a cigarette). *"See you later, alligator"* (I'm leaving). *"Tell them to do one"* (to get rid of someone).

- Non-specific spatio-temporal references: these are symbolic mechanisms that refer to reality, which is also undetermined or incredibly flexible.

  "See you in a bit" (later on, but undetermined). *"See you around"* (can express a desire to see someone at another time, in an undetermined location).

This use of non-literal language puts the symbolic ability of people on the spectrum to the test. The autistic person has to be constantly translating what neurotypical people say every x words. This is exhausting. Imagine having to constantly be translating what someone is saying as you're talking to each other. And, you also have to undertake this process in parallel, while you follow the conversation and get involved in it.

Let's take the example of a text written in a language that isn't our native language, but of which we do have a moderate level of knowledge. We start to read, but come across a word we don't understand. Mmmm, we'll write it down for now. We continue to read and the context gives us what we were missing in order to work out that word we hadn't understood. We go back to that paragraph and, at last, we understand it fully. We then go back to where we were. Suddenly, we come across a word we've never seen before. We have to stop and use a dictionary. We work out its meaning and continue reading. Shortly after, we come across a passage written using very technical language. Again, we have to stop to decipher the meaning before we can continue to read. We then come across a slang expression. We can't search for this in the dictionary, so we need to use other sources. We've ended up only reading 10 pages in an hour. We're exhausted and have to stop. Does the same thing happen when we read a text in our native language? Absolutely not.

So, this is the process of continuous translation, going forward and backwards non-stop, that an autistic person has to follow. In addition, if we're referring to a spoken conversation, face to face, they have to do this incredibly quickly and process lots of other things in parallel, as we've seen in chapter 5.

If you're on the spectrum, you might have become a master in these sorts of language tools over the years, and might even use some of them. But I'm sure that it has been a direct learning process: you hear an expression, look up its meaning, analysis it and then incorporate it into your speech. A neurotypical person can use expressions without knowing what they mean, and they might not ever take the time to look it up. This would be very unusual in the autistic community. Generally, someone on the spectrum would say: "Tell me exactly what you want to say". In children, their response is normally one of astonishment. And, as they grow up, they learn to hide this amazement, even though they haven't understood what they're being told. When it comes to adults, they often develop strategies to compensate for this 'incorrect' information, or lack of specificity.

> EVEN *A FLY* CAN THROW YOU OFF!

> A FLY? WHERE? *I CAN'T* SEE IT!

Excuse me?

"I got fed up of asking my friends to be more specific. I'm the annoying one who needs to know the exact time when we arrange to meet up. I end up saying "ok", but I feel something else inside" (Jaime, 36 years old)

When I was the Director of the Badajoz centre for autism, I was the tutor for the master's degree in autism that was taught in our centre. I put my students to the test. A fundamental aspect of working with the neurodivergent community is empathising with them in order to understand their needs and way (potentially very different) of perceiving reality. In order to get to this level of understanding of the condition, I proposed the following exercise: spend a day without using ultrametarepresentations in any conversations.

Before giving them permission to leave, in order to undertake this "empathetic experiment", I put them to the test with a few improvised conversations with me. They didn't last 5 seconds without "failing", even though they were really trying not to use these language tools. Why? Well, these are so rooted in our society that it's almost impossible not to sue them. Neurotypical people use this type of language automatically, without 'translating'. Someone on the spectrum can have a really hard time using a non-set phrase they don't understand. Autistic people who 'think in images' can rarely avoid creating this image in their mind, literally of course.

But, but...

I've been posting different images that demonstrate this exact symbolic exercise on my social media every Monday for a while now. People on the spectrum tend to find these drawings funny, and they can often have issues working out why it's funny, beyond its very literal meaning.

> **Tarta de cereza**
> @tartadecerezas
>
> Poca broma yo las visualizo en mi mente así 😂😂
>
> Daniel Millán López @dmillanlopez · 10h
> ¡Buenos días y feliz lunes! Vamos con ración doble de humor literal. 😜
>
> #TEA #CEA #ConoceTEA #ConoCEA #autismo #autista #asperger
>
> Y GRIEGA | I LATINA

Tweet[62] **by** @tartadecerezas. **Mondays call for literal humour.**

Going back to my experiment in Badajoz, my students were sweating buckets[63]. If they managed to go beyond the 5 minutes I'd say: "Imagine spending the entire day like that. And then imagine your whole life". And we're only talking about one, very specific aspect in the reality of autism. Add dichotomous thinking, executive dysfunction and theory of mind into the mix…. The effort people on the spectrum make to adapt to this world is so overwhelming, it comes as no surprise that many can't take this daily effort anymore and or they choose not to interact with other people.

---

[62] Jokes aside, I actually imagine them being like that
Good morning and happy Monday! It's time for some literal humour. GREEK Y. LATIN I

[63] Non-literal expression meaning "make a significant effort".

I mentioned creating prototypes when working on symbolic ability and language.

"The first tree my son saw is one that you can see out of the window at home. One day, we were wandering around another neighbourhood and I said: "Look son, that tree is huge". And he replied: "It's very big, but it isn't a tree. The tree is outside our window at home". (Jaime, autistic, 10 years old, talking to his dad).

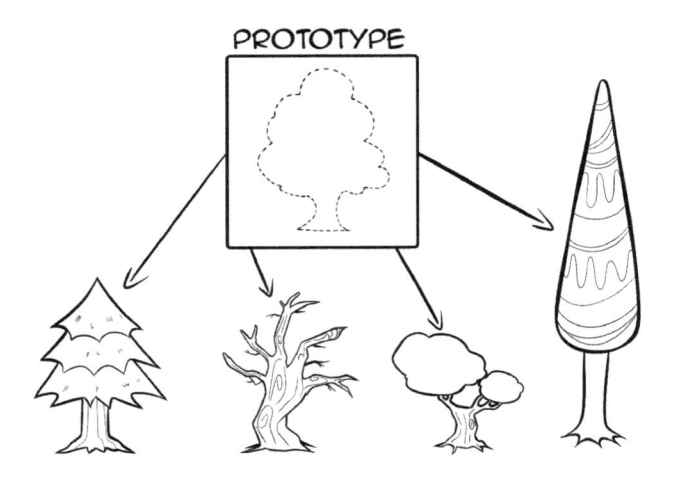

The creation of prototypes.

Because of their desire for specificity and coherence, people on the spectrum sometimes have difficulties creating these prototypes of each nominative category, each word or object. This process is learned almost intuitively in normative development. It's therefore not unusual for this to occur differently in a divergent maturity process, such as autism.

Let's go back to the example of the tree. Generally speaking, a neurotypical person doesn't have a clear, unambiguous example of every object they know and, if they do, it's very flexible and changeable. However, someone on the spectrum doesn't tend to create this same prototype. Instead, as the image thinker they tend to be, they have a clear and specific idea of each object, which can be transformed where necessary. We can say that the difference is that neurotypical people go from something very unspecific to something specific, whereas this process is the other way around in autism: from something very specific to the something less specific and variable.

"When I think of an object, I imagine a very clear, sharp image of it. When I was little, I struggled to break out of that mental inflexibility and even if the tiniest change was made to the image I had in mind, I'd say "It's not the same, it's similar, but it must be something else". Even today I sometimes struggle with that" (Lorena, 45 years old).

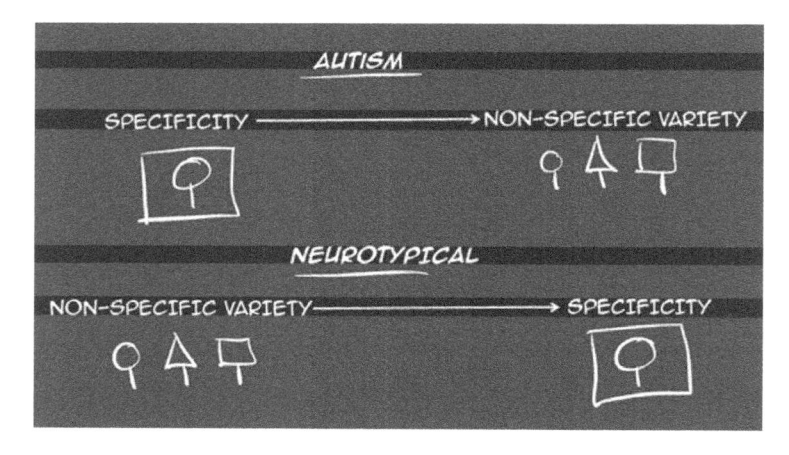

From specifics to non-specifics and vice versa. Two processing styles.

It's fundamental we understand the way someone processes before going ahead with any form of therapy or teaching.

Given that we know that autistic people use a different set of resources based on their specific brain configuration, communication mechanisms and strategies should be adapted in order to take advantage of these. This processing system fits in with deductive thinking, which enables the creation of rules from a specific reality. This is why sectors such as computing, where reality is able to be reproduced without significant variation, tend to be popular among autistic people. However, in the social environment, unspecific variety is so widespread that it inhibits them from creating set rules, or 'protocols of action' that adults on the spectrum so often request.

This can lead to challenges when it comes to generalisation in different areas. From not creating rules that can be generalised, to similar situations in which certain lessons can be employed in one context, but not in others. This explains why many of the lessons taught in consultations or schooling are not then later extrapolated to other situations and the need to work in real contexts, where possible.

Generalisation isn't my strong point.

There are situations in which the difficulties caused by non-literal language, which as we know also refer to spatio-temporal specificity, are more subtle and, therefore, harder for neurotypical people to anticipate and for autistic people to interpret.

In an online session with one of my young people, I asked him the following:

- *How's the piano going?*
- *Good, good…*
- *What was the last thing you played?*
- *Huh? Monopoly.*

It's incredibly common in neurotypical language to overlook these elements that are fundamental in order for an autistic person to construct a phrase correctly, or in this case, the question. This becomes complicated when we refer to an event in the past as opposed to something happening in the present.

- *Hi, Nicolás.*
- *Hi, Daniel.*
- *Nicolás, are your parents there? (He turns from one side and then the other).*
- *No, they're not here (confused look)*
- *I mean, are they at home?*
- *Oh, yes, they are. Hang on.*

As we've already mentioned, this symbolic ability is crucial when it comes to creating metarepresentations and these can be related both to play (creating alternative realities) or communication (pausing realities to create other new ones).

Some years ago, I created this table (see below) and adapted it for the Spanish population, based on the work of Gillbert and Peters (1995). In this table you'll find certain developmental milestones related to the appearance and evolution of language from just a few months of age to 5 years of age. The next two columns show these in terms of normative development and autistic development, where this development is very different to normotypical development (which tends to correspond to

Kanner or level 3 autism). Of course, this is not a 'set' table with no room for variation, as there can be exceptions and behaviours that are closer to one specific age range than another; even so, it's a starting point, especially for parents who might be unsure about their child's development.

AGE (MONTHS)	NEUROTYPICAL DEVELOPMENT	AUTISTIC DEVELOPMENT
2	- BABBLING - VOCAL NOISES	
6	- VOCAL CONVERSATIONS, TURN-TAKING AND RESPONSE	- CRIES THAT ARE DIFFICULT TO INTERPRET
8	- BABBLING WITH VARIED INTONATION - REPETITIVE SYLLABLES - FIRST POINTING GESTURES	- LIMITED OR "STRANGE" BABBLING - NO IMITATING OF SOUNDS, GESTURES OR EXPRESSIONS
12	- FIRST WORDS - GIBBERISH WITH INTONATION - LANGUAGE USED TO COMMENT - USE OF GESTURES TO GET ATTENTION, SHOW OBJECTS AND ASK QUESTIONS	- MAY SAY FIRST FEW WORDS, BUT MORE FOR SELF-STIMULATION - INTENSE CRYING, STILL DIFFICULT TO INTERPRET

Normotypical development and autistic development (Gillbert and Peters, 1995).

We now know that people on the spectrum reach milestones at different times, language being one of these. Many autistic people have developed language later than expected (perhaps even very late from a neurotypical perspective), and generally very abruptly, as is the case with other developmental milestones: sitting, standing, walking... In neurotypical development, it's unusual to develop elaborated language after 5 years of age. However, in autistic development this is frequent after this age or before the age expected in neurotypical development.

However, it's crucial to observe the child's development and develop a communication style, which doesn't have to be speech. What's important is that they have the most functional communicative tool possible and, consequently, reducing frustration and encouraging its use, we can work on oral language, but not as the sole or ultimate goal.

Alternative communication systems should aim for just that. These communication systems consist of a series of symbols or graphics used to communicate (intentional, spontaneous and generalised) and can be used alone, together with oral language, or as a means of support in order to stimulate or encourage it. The difference between symbol systems and sign language is that the first is developed and correspond to oral language, while this isn't the case in sign language. In autism, symbol systems are used, not sign language.

These alternative communication systems can be classified according to whether or not they use an aid. Those that use a support tend to use a visual aid, such as graphics or images (SPC, PECS, Bliss...), and those that don't have this type of aid, known as unaided, are gestural (For example, Benson-Schaeffer).

Choosing one support or another depends on the person's processing system, with special emphasis place, as you can imagine, on the symbolic field and other areas such as motor skills. Some "external" factors then come into play, as I'll explain below.

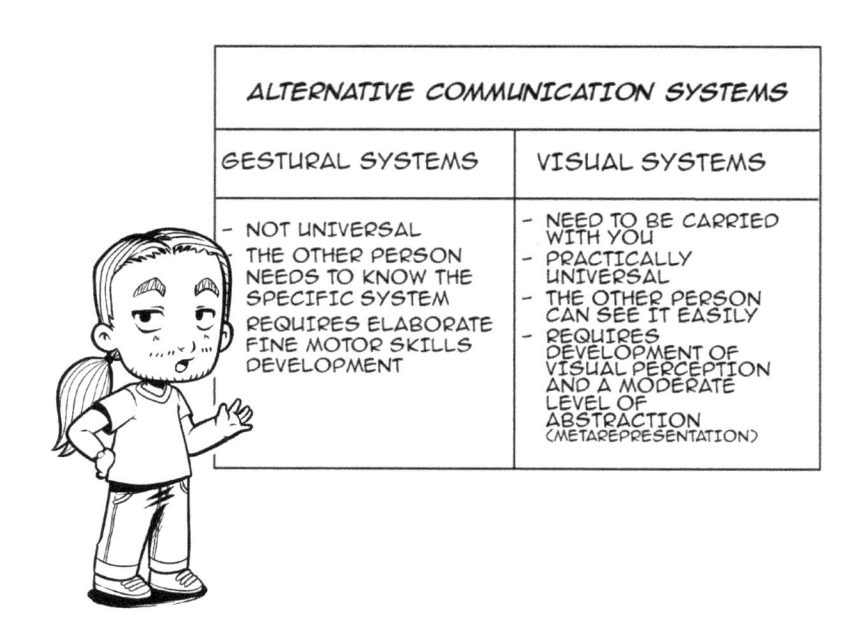

ALTERNATIVE COMMUNICATION SYSTEMS	
GESTURAL SYSTEMS	VISUAL SYSTEMS
- NOT UNIVERSAL - THE OTHER PERSON NEEDS TO KNOW THE SPECIFIC SYSTEM - REQUIRES ELABORATE FINE MOTOR SKILLS DEVELOPMENT	- NEED TO BE CARRIED WITH YOU - PRACTICALLY UNIVERSAL - THE OTHER PERSON CAN SEE IT EASILY - REQUIRES DEVELOPMENT OF VISUAL PERCEPTION AND A MODERATE LEVEL OF ABSTRACTION (METAREPRESENTATION)

Alternative communication systems.

Something that I find surprising and that amazes me, is that a system such as PECS (Picture Exchange Communication System), is recommended and employed at discretion within the autistic population, without having undertaken a prior analysis of the symbolic ability or considered other alternatives. In many cases, I'm sure the right system is chosen, but I've also come across people insisting on using this programme with young children who are not yet able to understand photographs as representations of reality, which makes it almost impossible for them to understand that a particular image corresponds to a particular action or object.

Personally, I think that picture exchange systems have two main down sides:

1) In cases where the objective is to stimulate language, they often fail because what the person on the spectrum understands is that communication is based on a mere exchange (in fact, this is where training begins), and they don't understand it as only 50% of what they have to do in order to ask for water, for example: search for water in their image library, give it to the adult and vocalise. The objective is achieved when all the steps are followed.

2) As their repertoire of objects and actions increases, the number of pictures they need to carry with them also increases.... Sometimes the mountains[64] of folders they have to carry around with them from one place to the next is truly ridiculous.

---

[64] Non-literal expression used to express "lots" or "a big pile" of something.

Yeah, really practical.

We often just assume an image, a photograph, a PECS is a visual system, but we forget that gestures are, too. Of course, although not permanent, they can be clearer and require less abstraction or ability to create metarepresentations.

Benson-Schaeffer's Total Communication programme is based on this same principle. It's generally applied to non-verbal children, with the clear intention to establish language. In my opinion this is questionable, given that the key is for the autistic person to have an effective communication tool, not for this to be spoken language.

It can be applied in cases in which, for whatever reason, communicative intentions are not observed. It's fundamental for the child to have a perception of stimulatory contingency (that relates mechanisms of cause and effect).

At the start of the programme, elements that can be very attractive for the child are used, as well as shaping[65] in order to learn the sign (in its three components: shape, positions and final movement) and linking back as learning principles. It's taught in natural contexts to facilitate the generalisation of learning,

Tips (for families of autistic children)

In terms of communicative intervention in children, the following variables should be taken into account:

> A) Communicative functions: we must be aware of the functions that regulate other people's behaviour; establish significant social interactions (quantity doesn't mean quality). In general, these functions are considered to not have been developed in autism, but this is an error: the reality is that the communicative functions are there, but their expression may not be adapted (or may not be as expected by other people) or they may be instrumental.
>
> There's a clear communicative intention in autism, but generally speaking, interaction:
>
> > 1) Is forced by adults when the child on the spectrum doesn't want to interact.

---

[65] Shaping is a psychological strategy used in order to increase the frequency of a particular behaviour in a person who does not do it, or does not do it as frequently as desired.

2) Failure in interaction causes rejection and leads to reluctancy to try again.

B) Development of increasingly sophisticated communicative means for each function. In order to do this, we must be very persistent, especially if we want to substitute behaviours that are dangerous either for the child or for the people around them, with others that are socially accepted (for example, instead of hitting themselves, they grab our hand to ask us for something). We need to improve the intelligibility of communicative means and develop the symbolic level of:

- Contact gestures (holding onto) to distal gestures (pointing).
- Descriptive gestures to symbolic gestures.
- Pre-symbolic sounds to words.

We need to use their communication styles to give them meaning, in order to reinforce them and encourage them to use them more: for example, to help them split their echolalias up into units and produce creative word combinations. We can use their repertoire and reinforce their communicative intention. We can then complicate the use of language later on.

C) Encourage reprocity in communication: developing the ability to participate in interactions involving turn-taking, in addition to the ability to value the information the other person needs in order to understand the message (see the chapter on theory of mind – ToM).

Tips for adults

The majority of the situations in which you may have difficulties with your surroundings when it comes to the symbolic field, will be linked to the lack of literal communication and specificity in what neurotypical people say.

As I've mentioned throughout this chapter, the use of non-literal language is so widespread in general that it's impossible to not come across it at some point in a conversation. On some occasions, there may not be a lapse in which you have to analyse an aspect of what the speaker has said, but when it occurs, it may cause anything from a processing delay (see chapter on information processing), to a potential block while you try and decipher the message. This type of situation can be incredibly frustrating, and it will also depend on what type of environment this interaction takes place in, in order to decide what to do.

"I feel stupid constantly asking what my work colleagues want to say, so I end up just not saying anything. Now I think either they think I'm mad or that something's wrong with me" (María, 29 years old).

In general, inaction is worse than asking, regardless of how annoying it may seem. The neurotypical mind is perverse and if it doesn't establish a communication pattern with which it feels comfortable, it soon starts to devise explanations, which can be absurd, for the lack of interaction of others.

In order for the neurotypical people who may be reading this book to understand the extent of this difficulty, let's use slang as an example. It's an aspect of non-literal language in itself, but you don't actually have any reason to understand it, even if it's in your native language. Suddenly, you hear an expression you don't understand, not even when contextualised, and you say: "excuse me, what?". It's possible that, even if translated literally, you don't understand it, as it requires significant immersion in the original cultural niche. This mental block can be continuous in an autistic person's mind.

When it comes to adolescents and young people, I tend to use a notebook in which we write down all the expressions that grab our attention and we apply them to different situations. This tends to be quite an attractive exercise and it gives them language resources that will later help them to interact with their peers and be more accepted by them.

A first attempt and putting what you've learned into practice.

Little by little we're creating a way of learning that will make its use more natural, taking into account (this is important) that it's never going to be automatic, so you should be aware of the effort you have to make as an autistic person. Don't force yourself to act like a neurotypical person at all times, just use the tools to achieve your goals, putting emphasis on who you are and how you act isn't wrong (how can someone say that being specific is wrong?), there are just other ways of proceeding that can offer benefits.

Of course, this doesn't mean to say that people on the spectrum are unable to use these metarepresentations. In fact, autistic people are also sarcastic and ironic, with an incredibly developed sense of humour. But putting the person in a context in which they don't expect certain metarepresentations and can't process this use of language so quickly (see chapter on processing in autism) and it takes them by surprise, is something else, for example. I want to emphasise this because this pretext is often used to invalidate diagnoses in some educational, clinical and healthcare contexts: "You can't be autistic, you've got a sense of humour".

"It happened during a meeting at work. We were super focused because we had to submit a project the next morning. Suddenly, one of my colleagues said: "I'm fed up, I'm going to grab a beer. Who's up for it?". Other colleagues said: "We are. Let's go!". I stood up angrily and said: "Are you actually going to just give up?". They all just looked at me.... Thinking about it now, it was clear they were joking, but I just didn't expect it at the time" (Daniel, 33 years old).

In other autistic people, however, the hyperrealistic perception of the world makes them escape at all costs[66]. Ultimately, as

---

[66] Non-literal expression that means "however possible".

we've mentioned, these suspensions of reality are no more than representations (misrepresentations) of it. This way, for these people on the spectrum, jokes or poetry might just not make sense. For Blanca, autistic and 40 years old: "I understand the mechanics of the joke, but I don't find it funny. Poetry doesn't make me feel the way it tries to. I can't lie, either. Honestly, a misinterpretation of something I've said and a lie are very similar. This is why I try not to leave things half-explained, so as not to give the wrong idea".

The wrong belief that autistic people don't have an imagination is just as widespread. This absurd statement has terrible implications, and if it were true (no autistic person could dedicate their life to creation nor fiction in that case) could be rooted in the concept of hyperrealism in people on the spectrum. But the difference revolves around the need for specifics, marking the limits of metrarepresentations, and tends to be ascribed to situations where logic and specific are preferrable. This doesn't mean to say that autistic people don't want to or can't use their imagination!

Regarding non-specifics in terms of time and space, in safe environments (family, friends) we should be able to request the specificity we need at any given time, no questions asked. Ultimately, when we go to the cinema, we're not going to a screening at 'in a while', we're going to one with a specific start time. Why can't we request other events are this specific? Similarly, when a situation is put off, we should try and rearrange when it can go ahead, giving a date and time, albeit approximate.

In work environments where not everyone chooses to make their condition known, and if we can't be ourselves, we can play the professionality card in order to request this specificity:

we can request it as a way in which to better perform in our role. When they say: "submit that piece of work when you can", we can demand an exact, specific submission date.

"At work, my supervisor sometimes said: "do that a bit better", referring to one of my tasks. Between the lack of specificity and my non-existent assertiveness, I spent days with my anxiety through the roof. I didn't know what to do, nor where to start. Now I know that I have the right to be told things specifically and I've learned to request that assertively" (Sonia, 28 years old).

Chapter 11

Sensitivity in autism

"When I'm really overwhelmed, even the sound of my own voice feels like stabbing pain in my ears, so I barely speak when that happens because I just can't take it. People tend to think I'm being disrespectful and not replying on purpose" (Laura, 29 years old).

Imagine this scenario: you go into a big shopping centre with a friend at peak time. As soon as the automatic doors open, you're hit by a series of sensations caused by a wave of different stimuli. Depending on the time of year, we can be hit by[67] either the air conditioning or the heating; both of which are always on full blast. At the same time, the visual impact can be huge, too: there's so much intense lighting wherever you look. Also, every shop has different lights, some of which are neon, others flash, others have animated messages that scroll by... The lights are totally overwhelming. On top of the roar of all the shoppers, who are talking at the top of their voices, the music is unmissable. And, of course, each shop has its own playlist blaring out the door, making the background noise a

---

[67] Non-literal expression used to describe a sudden change, in this case, in temperature.

dense and indigestible cocktail. There are all types of smells; from the smell of the disinfectant used to mop the floors, to the perfume shop 100 metres from the entrance. You can also smell all the sweaty people around us. People going about their business all over the place. Some wandering around aimlessly, others on a mission. There doesn't appear to be any order like on the roads, where - almost everywhere- drives on the right. But, for some bizarre reason, almost nobody bumps into any-one else. It's a sort of organised chaos.

Everyone experiences this to some extent, regardless of whether or not they're autistic, as soon as they change context and they start to receive multiple sensory stimuli. However, the processing difference in people on the spectrum is abysmal when compared to those of neurotypical people, and even more so in these specific circumstances.

When it comes to autism, it's essential we know how this information, these stimuli, are processed. We'll continue with the shopping centre scenario. The autistic person has just gone inside with their friend. Their friend is neurotypical, after saying "Aargh, it's packed in here" and maybe complaining about the noise, appears to go straight back to being relaxed, while the person on the spectrum seems to have been anchored in the initial state of shock after going into the huge building.

Welcome to Hell.

While they walk, the neurotypical friend begins to say something to their autistic friend. It's not that the autistic friend can't hear them, but they can't hear what they're saying clearly. Their words get lost in the chaos of lights, smells and other sounds that feel like they're hitting them in the head. When the friend realises they're not responding, they say, even louder: "What's wrong with you? Can't you hear me?". The autistic person responds: "Don't shout at me, I'm not deaf! I just can't concentrate in here….".

So, what's going on? Let's see what the studies say. Some mention people on the spectrum as having 'exaggerated' response patterns to stimuli because of very high arousal levels[68] (Hirstein et al., 2001; Volkmar et al., 2005). This explanation seems insufficient to me. It's true that due to previous experiences (or in response to uncertainty, remember the need for anticipation), the person on the spectrum finds themselves hyper alert in certain contexts, but basing the explanation for their sensory response on a pre-emptive mechanism doesn't seem right to me.

Another explanation, this time seen widely in literature on autism, is the presence of patterns that are hyper and hyporeactive to different stimuli. The experiments undertaken have been predominantly based on these two response patterns as regards touch, light and sound (Barenek, 2006). Some studies have also focused on the presence of a mixed sensitivity pattern (hyper and hypo) in a single person.

Within this paradigm, the patterns of hyper and hypo stimulation are understood according to the behavioural response of the person on the spectrum and not on the underlying processes behind this response. They are therefore descriptions of behaviours according to a sensory profile. For example, within the noted studies by Baranek, a style of hyper-response due to lack of attention paid to 'new' sounds is described. Is it really a sensory regulation issue? Or could we be talking about the infamous paradoxic hearing loss?[69], where someone on the spectrum only pays attention to stimuli they deem functional.

---

[68] Arousal or level of cortical awakening is a term used in neurology, physiology and psychology that denotes a general physiological and psychological awakening (Wikipedia).

[69] Paradoxic hearing loss is the apparent lack of response to being called or instructions, without any hearing issues being present. However, the person dos respond to a different series of auditory stimuli.

The way I see it, what's happening is more along the lines of studies by Tecchio (2003) regarding difficulties in sensory discrimination, but with certain nuances, or what was described previously by Williams (1994) when stating that: "the brain only consciously processes one modality, whereas subconsciously, an unknown quantity of information can enter". The ability to capture and process information from different sources is known as 'polytropic', while, if only one channel is processed, this is 'monotropic'. Many people on the spectrum have referred to this mono-processing in order to explain their information processing preferences: if they have to be aware of too many channels, there's too much information and they become overwhelmed. Again, sequential versus parallel processing (see chapter 5).

In my opinion, the problem isn't so much the mechanisms that collect these stimuli (the senses), but their superior processing (at a cortical level): this is what I like to call the funnel hypothesis. When our senses begin to capture all these stimuli, an information transmission phase occurs in our nervous system, via different parts of the brain, followed by a sensory integration process. At this time, the brain analyses the information, that which is most relevant, or not, according to a hierarchy of priorities. This process establishes the degree of relevance of each bit of information and places it in order of priority.

When the different stimuli continue to arouse our receptors and the information continues to be received by the brain, this is processed at a superior attention level, or not, depending on the level of importance our system has given it.

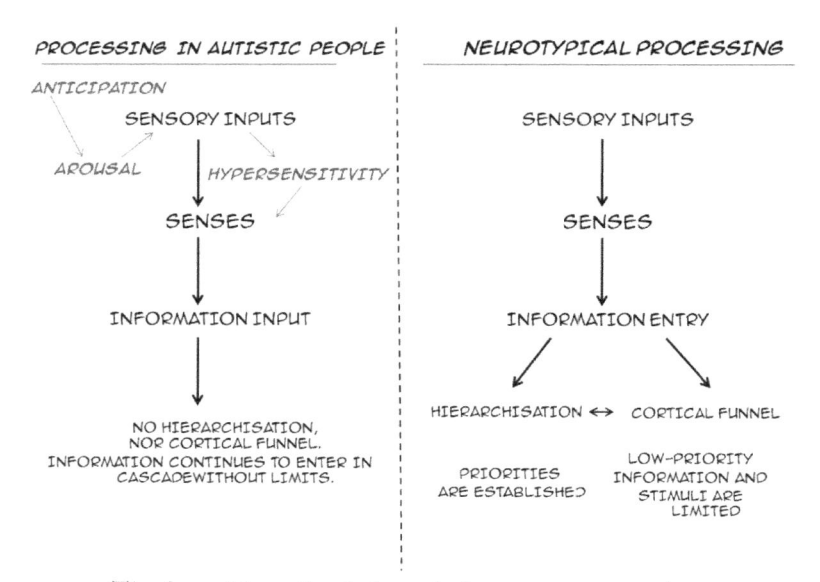

```
PROCESSING IN AUTISTIC PEOPLE          NEUROTYPICAL PROCESSING

ANTICIPATION
      ↘   SENSORY INPUTS                    SENSORY INPUTS
   ↙   ↓   ↘                                      ↓
 AROUSAL    HYPERSENSITIVITY
            ↓                                     ↓
          SENSES                               SENSES
            ↓                                     ↓
     INFORMATION INPUT                    INFORMATION ENTRY
            ↓                                ↙         ↘
                                    HIERARCHISATION ↔ CORTICAL FUNNEL
    NO HIERARCHISATION,
    NOR CORTICAL FUNNEL.                                LOW-PRIORITY
  INFORMATION CONTINUES TO ENTER IN      PRIORITIES   INFORMATION AND
      CASCADE WITHOUT LIMITS.          ARE ESTABLISHED   STIMULI ARE
                                                          LIMITED
```

The funnel hypothesis in autistic sensory processing.

In the shopping centre example, a hierarchy is established, and the smells, background music and shouting voices are placed on an inferior priority level in a neurotypical brain. This allows them to focus on what their brain considers priority: where they're walking to and the conversation with their autistic friend.

However, this doesn't mean to say that the other signals are completed 'blocked'. This means that the information is still there in the sense that the stimuli are still being captured, but it's as if they were simmering away on a back burner.[70] At any time, they could pay attention to a specific stimulus categorised as low priority and place it at the top of the hierarchy and

---

[70] Non-literal expression used to describe something being present, but not priority.

process it as deeply as possible. This results in the amount of information regarding these stimuli that access the person's consciousness being 'funnelled', enabling them to process what is really relevant, intensely (or actively).

For a person on the spectrum, the start of this process is already different for two reasons:

A) They've probably experienced a nervous anticipation prior to the event, in expectation of an unpleasant situation due to their experience. If there was no anticipation, there could be an impact of unpredictability. In both cases, a high level of sensory activation occurs.

B) If the person already identifies themselves to have hypersensitivity of certain senses, the intensity of the entrance of the information will be greater initially.

As you can see, this paradigm consists of the two theoretical explanations most widely employed in terms of studying sensory patterns in autism we mentioned not long ago, but we take it one step further and place them as just elements prior to this one.

The entry of the information via the sensory receptors is nothing short of torrential. It arrives very quickly, via multiple channels, but while the neurotypical person doesn't need more than about two minutes to get used to it, the autistic person continues to capture all the stimuli with the same level of intensity and, even more importantly, with the same level of priority. For some reason, the brain doesn't act as a 'funnel' and considers all stimuli to be equally relevant. It's therefore impossible for them to focus on their friend's conversation, because although they can hear fine, their brain deems their voice as important as the background music or the screams of a child playing 30 metres away.

The sequential processing and difficulties processing quickly and establishing a hierarchy of stimuli, together with stimulatory hyperfocus, could be the basis for this supposed sensory dysfunction or dysregulation.

So, how does it feel when this 'dysregulation' occurs? Autistic people experience this in many different ways, but as you'll know if you're autistic (or if as a neurotypical person you were able to empathise with this particular example), they tend to be incredibly unpleasant. Some people describe this overwhelm as being like a giant stone on top of their brain, causing them dreadful migraines. Others describe noises with feelings of physical pain. Some autistic people also experience this differently if the noise is high or low-pitched. The variety is incredible, but with one common denominator, which is by no means trivial.

"I've spent the morning in a huge shopping centre packed with people, and I realised I was becoming overwhelmed when I felt the need to hide inside an IKEA wardrobe" (Andrea, 26 years old).

It's very common for children to cover their ears. In fact, this image has become an idiosyncrasy of autism in children, hasn't it? I'm still amazed by the ordinary nature of how people describe these situations, as if autistic kids cover their ears because they feel like it. In some cases, this behaviour doesn't achieve its goal, which is to escape from this/those stimuli that are causing them pain, and they can even start to desperately hit their head in an attempt to stop the horrible sensation they're experiencing. If we continue to use this 'iconic' image, we should at least understand where it comes from. And, more importantly, we should do something about it.

According to Bill Nason (2011), hypersensitivity in autism can be the cause of multiple responses, such as meltdowns, shutdowns, self-stimulation and hetero-aggressive and self-aggressive behaviours.

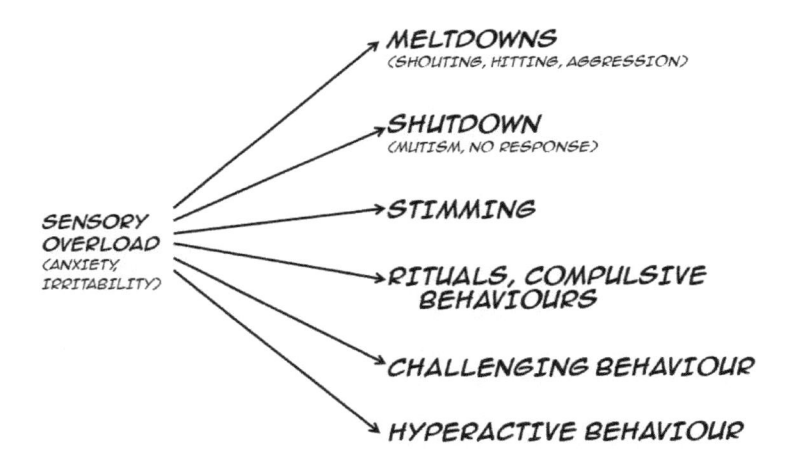

```
                          ┌→ MELTDOWNS
                          │   (SHOUTING, HITTING, AGGRESSION)
                          │
                          ├→ SHUTDOWN
                          │   (MUTISM, NO RESPONSE)
SENSORY                   │
OVERLOAD ─────────────────┼→ STIMMING
(ANXIETY,                 │
IRRITABILITY)             ├→ RITUALS, COMPULSIVE
                          │   BEHAVIOURS
                          │
                          ├→ CHALLENGING BEHAVIOUR
                          │
                          └→ HYPERACTIVE BEHAVIOUR
```

Behaviour in response to sensory overload. Bill Nason (2011)

Stimming is another of the signs most commonly associated with the autistic condition, however, as I mentioned in chapter 5, they aren't exclusive to it. Despite this, they've been the source of inappropriate therapies[71], so as not to say cruel, throughout the years and even today. Foxx and Azrin (1973)

---

[71] Capilla et al. (1989) frame stimming alongside aggression, self-harm, hyperactivity and tantrums as the most frequent problematic behaviours in autism.

suggested different methods to eliminate these behaviours, as they considered them "potentially harmful". Some authors believe that stimming is the essence of "pointless behaviours" (Zinner, 2010), or "[…] a behaviour that occurs in a specific way, with abnormal connotations" (Sambraus, 1985). This could not be further from the truth, and this perspective maintains a faithful reflection of the archaic and absurd paradigm of viewing autism and autistic people as incapable of controlling their own activity. Labelling a misunderstood action as useless or absurd is out of order, and a clear example of the lack of empathy of some researchers.

I often receive tales of contexts in which an autistic child has been forced to "stop doing that movement, because it isolates them from their surroundings". The situation wouldn't be as serious if this message wasn't coming from therapists supposedly specialised in developmental disorders. Redirecting this stim or other (similar) action to something more functional or delaying it on occasions where it could interfere with learning is different, but in these contexts, there is another series of important processes and considerations to take into account.

Stimming is nothing other than a means of regulating emotions and activation. These can be anything from the infamous 'flapping', hand clapping, jumping, rocking movements or they can be verbal, with the repetition of different sounds without an intention to communication, as they are exclusively stimulatory. There's nothing bad about them, as long as the person doesn't hurt themselves or others when doing it. They're not that different from what neurotypical children and adults do. Who doesn't shake their leg up and down when they're sat down and feeling nervous? Who doesn't repeatedly flick their pen when they're studying, for example? The difference here is that these movements are 'socially acceptable'. The fact that even harmful behaviours such as nail biting (onychophagy) seem to be more acceptable than a child rocking backwards and forwards, is absurd. At the end of the day, stimming is just a scapegoat[72] used to recognise that people don't know how to interact with people on the spectrum, especially as children, and it highlights stimming as an interaction 'blocking mechanism'. And, preventing the person on the spectrum from stimming is taking away what might be their only defence mechanism.

Stimming is a regulatory mechanism that helps autistic people deal with sensory sensitivity. In fact, hyper focusing on their stimming can help them, reducing the surge of sensory stimuli that overwhelm them. Rhythmic patterns can help to regulate the nervous system and, therefore, repetitive stimming patterns can help people with proprioception difficulties be more aware of their own body and sensations.

The percentages that determine the number of people on the spectrum who have some form of sensitivity are huge. Some studies highlight that more than half the autistic population have some type of 'sensory difficulty', while other studies ensure that almost 95% have some form of sensory processing disorder (TPS, as described by Jean Ayres in 1972). The review of these studies and the increase in this percentage appears to have a correlation to the inclusion of auditory sensitivity in the sample, in detriment to another type of sensitivity. A coincidence?

---

[72] "Scapegoat" is used to refer to an innocent person or group singled out for blame (Wikipedia).

Logically, the different types of sensitivity in autism are derived from the sensory channel that captures each stimulus, and can be broken down as follows:

- Auditory sensitivity: saturation in certain, intense environments (multiple sound stimuli) or due to sudden or continuous loud noises. The act of autistic children covering their ears is indicative of this potential sensitivity. As regards this specific type of sensitivity, it's very important to analyse the unpredictability patterns (executive dysfunction) in addition to multiple processing difficulties.

"When I go out, I always take my noise-cancelling headphones with me. They're a must, more so than my keys or phone. They help me to focus on the important things, otherwise it's just impossible for me" (Amaia, 23 years old).

- Visual sensitivity: in general, this tends to be associated with the impossible nature of keeping your eyes open in contexts with incredibly intense lighting. This can occur with natural light, artificial light, or both. On other occasions, visual stimuli searching can occur, such as different light sources or patterns.

"I can't stand sunlight, even when it's cloudy, so I wear sunglasses at all times. Sometimes it happens indoors. People look at me weirdly, so I assume they think I'm being disrespectful. I've been to the doctors and the opticians, but they can't find an explanation. They said my eyes are fine" (Sonia, 40 years old).

- Tactile sensitivity (sometimes called somatic or haptic): this is the sensory channel in which it's most common to see patterns of hypersensitivity (dislike of certain fabrics, aversion to touch) and hyposensitivity (difficulty perceiving certain tactile stimuli or temperature). It's closely linked to hyperfocus and, in aversion to touch, social factors.

"I can't stand labels on t-shirts. I can always feel them. Always. Sometimes they feel like a razor blade" (Marcos, 34 years old).

"I don't like hugging people, nor them hugging me. I don't like the feeling of pressure on my body. I don't know what the protocol is either, how long a hug should last, for example. It makes me feel very anxious" (Blanca, 39 years old).

- Olfactory sensitivity: from the incredibly high perception of different smells (hyper) to difficulty identifying certain smells (hipo), or at least when the stimuli is first encountered[73].

"They've always said the same about my sense of smell: 'You're pregnant', and I was always afraid of being pregnant because I thought: "Bloody hell, being able to smell even more is going to be unbearable". And luckily, I didn't notice a difference in my sense of smell whether I was pregnant or not" (Lara, 33 years old).

- Taste sensitivity: intrinsically linked to the previous type for obvious reasons. In this case we're talking about intolerance of different textures, as there's as much texture variety as there are different types of foods. Important: as with olfactory sensitivity, take into account any potential digestive issues, which appear to be

---

[73] A study by Baron-Cohen in 2012 stated that people on the spectrum need more time to process olfactory stimuli "adequately". This study was then replicated in Japan in 2019 (Kumazaki et al.), with similar results.

common in people on the spectrum[74]. It's also very important to analyse whether or not it's an issue with hyper selectivity in terms of shape or colour, for example:

"For me, the texture of seafood is as if I was eating plasticine. I can't stand chewing it. I don't like the combinations of certain ingredients. For example, I love fruit, but I cannot eat a fruit salad" (Irene, 31 years old).

- Vestibular sensitivity and proprioception: these are defined separately as part of the interoceptive senses, and are both named exteroceptive. The vestibular system is involved in corporal balance as a whole, or in specific parts of the body. Responsible for sitting and standing, for example.

In autism 'strange' or 'weird' postures are common when sitting on a chair or lying on a bed. Sitting upright can be a problem at times, so it's not unusual to see an autistic person leaning a part of their body on an element or object. However, for some authors (Gray, Attwood and Holliday-Wulley, 1999), this 'unusual' posture forms part of the diagnostic criteria for Asperger's syndrome.

"I'm always twisting my ankles and hitting my shoulders on the door frames. But I'm actually really good at some sports because I can have good coordination. I don't understand it" (Marina, 35 years old).

The incredible variety of sensory reaction, mixed reactivity and the fact that someone can present fluctuations, in other words, they sometimes present hyper or hyperreaction, makes this a

---

[74] There are very varied studies regarding the prevalence of gastrointestinal issues among the autistic population. Sometimes the samples analysed do not consider determining factors such as food aversions.

very complex aspect within the reality of autism. Many more studies are required in order to reach a correct description. Today, the DSM5 includes this aspect in the diagnostic criteria, but very superficially (according to the manual itself: "[…] the examples are illustrative, but not exhaustive").

Card collection. Which ones have you got?

In any case, sensitivity in autism must be taken into account, albeit associated with negative reactions by those who perceive stimuli with too much or too little intensity, there are also examples of very positive and evocative experiences.

"I'm addicted to my partner's smell. Sometimes I tell him not to wash. I don't like him to smell bad, it's not that, I just like his natural smell, no soap, no perfumes of aftershave. The same thing happens with my baby. When I smell them it's like a feeling of total climax and relaxation. Sometimes I feel like smelling them and I crave it if I can't" (Sonia, 31 years old).

According to the Spanish Society of Paediatric Neurology (SENEP, 2019), between 44% and 80% of children on the spectrum have a wide range of sleep disorders. This percentage is marginally higher than in cases of ADHD, for example, where the percentage is between 20% and 70%. In neurotypical children, there's a more significant difference and the interval ranges between 25% and 44% (Idiazábal y Aligas-Martínez, 2009). The information we have regarding autistic adults isn't as abundant as in children, but it appears that these sleep difficulties are maintained, despite maturation: "The sudden remission of sleep problems in the neurotypical population is 52.4% compared to just 8.3% in autism" (Pin, 2019).

It has been known for some time now that there are several neurotransmitters involved in the sleep-wake cycle (gaminobutyric acid (GABA), serotonin and melatonin). Specifically: "Melatonin is considered to be the sleep hormone and is used in ASD to improve sleep onset and decrease night-time awakenings. Autism has been associated with a decreased melatonin secretion in the evening. It produces few side effects, with the exception of daytime sedation in some cases (Hervás, et al., 2011). However, the single study of these chemical factors and the introduction of melatonin as a treatment does not seem to hold the key to regulating sleep in children on the spectrum (Reynolds and Malow, 2011). On the other hand, behavioural intervention mechanisms, such as pictograms that show the process of going to bed, do appear to lead to substantial improvement (Papadopoulos et al., 2015).

In addition to neurological factors, another series of environmental factors influence the quality of sleep to some extent but, in all cases, diverse studies conclude that the causes are multifactorial. Can sensitivity patterns in autism be contributing to sleep difficulties? As we've seen in this chapter, it's more than likely this is the case.

The two combinations of factors with the greatest influence and over which we have certain control, according to Gonzalo Pin-Arboledas (2019) are sleep pressure and sleep hygiene.

- Sleep pressure refers to someone's "real" need for rest. The more hours of wakefulness (the time we spend awake), the greater the sleep pressure. Therefore, the more sleep pressure, the easier it is it initiative. In accordance with Gonzalo Pin: "People with ASD have less sleep pressure, and it doesn't coincide with circadian rhythms".

- Sleep hygiene refers to all circumstances that may interfere when falling and staying asleep, such as what we consume, and the environmental and sensorial circumstances prior to going to bed.

If we think about the amount of stimulation and overstimulation a person can experience in the minutes and hours before going to bed, and if we go back to the cortical funnel hypothesis and the lack of priority hierarchy, it's reasonable to think that this overstimulation could also have a negative impact, both in children and adults, when it comes to going to sleep. This is why parents often tell the same story: kids who are literally exhausted, but they "can't stop thinking about other things". The hierarchical pressure the proprioceptive system can put on the hierarchisation of tiredness is not greater than the other sensations.

This is why ensuring good sleep hygiene is even more important for autistic people than for neurotypical people. As regards the sensory component of sleep hygiene, the number of stimuli to be processed should be limited, avoiding the use of devices that omit blue light (phones, tablets, etc) and, in any case, undertake activities that prioritise sequential processing as opposed to parallel processing, and reduce auditory and visual stimulation (noises, artificial lights in general). Another series of procedures (such as the use of weighted blankets, for example), as not proven to be generally effective and depend on the sensory pattern of each individual (Gringras et al., 2014).

The sensory overwhelm and persistent anxiety experienced by many autistic people as a result of multiple conflicts in their surroundings appear to form the basis of the difficulties encountered by autistic people in terms of sleep. These start at a very young age and, as expected (as sensory and social conflicts are not resolved), continue into adulthood. In my experience, I've often found a very unpleasant sleep disorder known as sleep paralysis to be associated with anxiety and meltdowns (see chapter 13).

Well, I don't really know what to say…

Sleep paralysis is a type of sleep disorder associated with the REM phase (rapid eye movement). The REM sleep phase it when the brain is most active, but the brain stem appears to block the motor neurons. We experience the most vivid and extensive dreams during this phase.

During sleep paralysis, the person loses the ability to speak and voluntarily move their head, thorax or extremities due to a total loss of muscle tone. The duration is variable and can last from just a few seconds, to minutes. It's a truly disturbing experience, and makes you feel totally defenceless. In fact, the anxiety it causes is so great that cases of visual hallucinations (sounds, shadows of people, difficulty breathing and strangling sensation, extracorporeal perception) have been recorded. This paralysis tends to occur when the REM sleep phase occurs in the waking up times, and is the reason why corporal paralysis occurs. This sleep disorder is generally diagnosed by way of various tests, such as the Multiple Sleep Latency Test (MSLT) or polysomnography.

The significant prevalence of altered sleep patterns and different sensitivity and perception patterns in autism appears to make people on the spectrum more susceptible to suffering this type of disorder, which is, without a doubt, associated with both internal and external factors such and anxiety, a comorbid condition persistent in autism (see chapter 13). The treatment prescribed tends to be pharmacological. In my experience, I've found that a behavioural intervention aimed at reducing levels of anxiety and generating more awareness of the perceptive system is more effective in the long term.

Tips

The various strategies to improve the environmental conditions for autistic children tend to be divided into sensory stimulation and sensory integration strategies, as they are two different processes. The first aims to get the person used to the presence of the stimulus that overwhelms them (or that doesn't completely activate them) and the second promotes the selective detection of stimuli, their discrimination (if relevant or not) and the adequate response. This type of training tends to be undertaken by professionals in occupational therapy, in stimulation rooms.

Beyond the recreational interest produced in this type of stimulations (applied in adapted playrooms and focused on the child's interests) and the physical energy required by many of the activities and, therefore, the emotional well-being they provide, my query is to do with the generalisation of what is learned to other contexts in which, although slightly, the stimulatory conditions are modified. Sometimes I come across programmes (or better said, lack of) in these interventions that should really set alarm bells off. This can be extended to any intervention with very general goals and a lack of precision as regards the steps to be followed in order to achieve them, or there are no estimates regarding results. Very general goals such as 'improve interaction' or 'improve communication' are incredibly vague and don't allow us to establish a reasonable judgment as regards the effectiveness of the therapies themselves.

The conclusions reached by the studies undertaken on the effectiveness of this intervention style for autistic children are questionable. The majority of the studies undertaken offer a very positive perspective in terms of improvements in the effectiveness of social interaction, play and day-to-day activities, but not in all cases (Pfeiffer et al. 2008). An additional issue is that sometimes these interventions are focused on (as if this were the ultimate goal) the reduction of stimming (Zisserman, 1992) and the increase in attention span, without focusing on whether or not the activity is functional for the child on the spectrum (Hinojosa, 2001), which is essential, as we saw in chapter 6.

The majority of occupational therapies related to autism are focused on autistic children. There are very few strategies for adults, despite the fact that the personal accounts from people on the spectrum offer, in my opinion, much more accurate information than the neurological studies or questionnaires for parents in terms of making significant changes. In this case we have the works of the renowned Temple Grandin or other biographical collections by Gerland (2003).

"My hearing is as if I'm wearing a hearing aid with the volume stuck on "super high". It's like a microphone that picks up absolutely everything. I've got two options: switch the microphone on and overwhelm myself with so much noise, or switch it off" (Temple Grandin).

As is the case in children, for adults the most common sensitivity is auditory. In these cases, I recommend working on several areas:

1) The first is anticipation. Familiarity with the context you're going to encounter will help to reduce anxiety and the arousal that could lead to perceptive chaos will decrease. Today, thanks to technology, we can even estimate how many people will be in certain public places, see 3D images of the location or take virtual tours.

   > Jai
   > @AutieAcademic
   >
   > Hoy me toca ir al dentista y lo odio. Han reformado la clínica. Es como ir a un sitio desconocido. Acabo de ver que han publicado un video de cómo es, desde entrar por la puerta hasta salir. No se dan cuenta pero los detalles así son una maravilla. Anticipación! #soyautista

   Tweet[75] by @AutieAcademic. Anticipation, anticipation, anticipation.

2) Whenever you anticipate you're going to be faced with auditory saturation, wear passive noise-cancelling headphones. Active cancelling is effective too, but only for

---

[75] I have a dentist appointment today and I'm dreading it. They've renovated the clinic. It's like going somewhere completely new. I've just noticed they've uploaded a video tour; from the moment you go through the door until you leave. They won't have realised, but this makes a world of difference. Anticipation! #soyautista

very constant, specific sounds (the hum of an airport, for example).

3) Undertake therapeutic auditory discrimination and hierarchisation activities in controlled contexts, so as to later apply these to real contexts. Although there is little scientific evidence of significant improvements, even in cases where the methods are followed strictly (again, generalisation can work against us). I'm not referring to Tomatis[76] or SENA[77] methods of course, which don't have any scientific validity.

The perception of sounds that other people don't generally perceive is very common. The mention of sounds or buzzing coming from certain electronic devices is particularly notable.

"I hear noises all day, such as the fridge, and the electricity running through the walls. I tell my wife about it and she says well, you can only hear it if you listen out for it. I can't not hear it, it's just always there" (Francisco 49 years old).

In terms of sensitivity related to the vestibular system, we normally come across two different circumstances in adults.

1) The first tends to be related to corporeal posture, especially when the person is sitting or lying down. These postures are considered "weird" by the autistic person themselves. Beyond the superficial social branding of sitting in a strange position, these are consequences

---

[76] The Tomatis method is a therapy based on music therapy, which aims to improve skills in autism, beyond speech control.
[77] The SENA method (Neuro-Auditory Stimulation System) is a computer software that supposedly improves diverse skills in multiple conditions or disorders.

that occur especially beyond certain ages when sitting in these postures.

The fact that many people on the spectrum struggle with gross motor skills isn't much help here either.

Correcting posture when walking, sitting or lying down can help save us lots of visits to traumatology and physiotherapists. I'd personally recommend sports (of any kind), because of all the benefits it offers, not just in terms of posture.

> 2) Many autistic people find using weighted blankets and objects that help them reduce stimulatory overwhelm very relaxing[78]. In my experience, this strategy doesn't work for everyone. In general, it tends to be more effective in autistic people who are able to hyperfocus. Being able to hyperfocus on the tactile stimulatory sensation and undergo a sequential process of the sensations seems to offer a calming effect, releasing endorphins that help us to relax.

In terms of visual sensitivity, most studies are focused on how the perception of this sense affects communication and the purpose of the activity. Even so, there are some interesting studies that show that approximately 30% of people on the spectrum have some form of photosensitivity (Schultz, Klin and Jones, 2011) and, as we know, this really can't be remedied in any way other than prevention. Some procedures, such as the Irlen method or behavioural optometry offer very contradictory results as regards their effectiveness (Cotton and Evans, 1990).

---

[78] A similar concept to Temple Grandin's famous "Hug Machine". Not to be confused with the aversive "forced hug" therapy, which is just abuse.

As regards tactile sensitivity, as we've highlighted previously, social interactions play a key role in determining the overall scope and there generally tends to be a combination of these factors. Many autistic people face significant difficulties finding materials and textures they feel comfortable with and sometimes they have to use powerful fabric softeners in order to wear certain items of clothing. Footwear tends to be another additional challenge: some shoes can cause terrible pain beyond the discomfort a neurotypical person may experience while wearing the same pair. Similarly, when an autistic person experiences tactile sensitivity together with other hypersensitivities, sex can be an overwhelming experience.

"I'm one of those autistic people that has certain issues when it comes to physical contact with other people (probably due to my hypersensitivity. Brushing against me can be as painful as if it were sand paper. But it can also give me unbelievable pleasure. It's difficult to deal with this intensity, and sharing it with others is even harder" (Montse – AsperRevolution, 35 years old).

Interoception is the perception of signals that come from inside of our body, as opposed to from outside or other external factors. According to Mahler (2015), sensory receptors on the inside of our body process multiple signals that can be anything from temperature perception or heart rate to feelings of hunger, thirst or needing to go to the toilet. Again, in autism these perceptions tend to have either a hypo or hyper response. The most common is for autistic children and adults who don't 'feel' enough to perceive necessities. Autistic adults often mention forgetting to eat during the day because they don't feel hunger, or they forget to go to the toilet.

"I can go for hours, perhaps even an entire day, without really feeling the need to go to the toilet. In the end, when I do go, mostly by obligation, it

turns out my bladder was full. Now I use an app that notifies me and I go when it tells me to" (María, 26 years old).

In order to work on these areas, the key is creating a clear, immediate backup plan. The strategies generally used in these cases aren't that effective because they don't consider this basic principle of autism. We can use an application that notifies us that we should go to the toilet or drink water every so often, for example. The next step is to concentrate on that sensation, but only when we're focused on it. This allows us to force our interoceptive mechanisms to work harder to send signals to make us more aware of this sensation and, consequently, act accordingly.

Some researchers (Johnson, 2013) suggest that patterns of hypersensitivity in autism are responsible for the fact that a significant percentage of autistic people are also synaesthetic. Synaesthesia is a sensory phenomenon (although, it's also a rhetoric figure) in which sensations corresponding to a different sense are perceived, at the same time as perceiving a certain stimulus via the sensory channel designed for this purpose. Synaesthetic people experience perception associated with others (between two or multiple senses); for example, colours are associated to certain letters or different shapes if they see or think in odd or even numbers, of experiences taste sensations associated with different types of music, for example. On a cerebral level, this implies a connection between various areas of the brain that wouldn't ordinarily be connected. Therefore, the activation of one of the perceptive channels automatically activates the other.

Studies by Baron-Cohen (2013) found that approximately a third of people on the spectrum presented synaesthetic patterns. Specifically, associations were reported between different letters of the alphabet that evoked different colours, different visual experiences associated with sounds and different colours triggered by different olfactory stimuli.

Some hypotheses as to why this phenomenon is more common in people on the spectrum suggests the perception of details and hyperfocus as a probable cause of the development of synaesthetic patterns (Hänggi et al., 2011). Other studies, however, suggest the local brain connectivity hypothesis (Dovern 2012) or the presence of high levels of serotonin in early childhood (Brogaard, 2013). Regardless of the origin or origins of this phenomena, many years of study lie ahead in order to better understand its genesis, as is the case with the different sensitivity patterns in autism. According to Dr. Berit Brogaard: "[…] we still do not have enough data to reach firm conclusions".

To bring this chapter to an end, I want to continue to talk about prosopagnosia, the phenomenon I mentioned at the beginning of this book, when I told you the story of why I chose to specialise in autism. Agnosia – or face blindness – is a common characteristic in autism, but it doesn't occur in all cases (Blackburn, 1999). People with prosopagnosia have difficulties recognising other people's faces, and therefore, identifying and distinguishing between people. It varies in intensity, and it's generally more common in people on the spectrum with a more prominent image processing.

People with prosopagnosia need to make an incredible effort in order to be able to recognise other people: in general, they focus on details such as whether or not the person wears glasses, their hairstyle or clothing. But, of course, this strategy works on the assumption that these people maintain a relatively similar and stable aesthetic. Other studies state that, as expected, there's a positive correlation between prosopagnosia with difficulty identifying facial expressions and emotions (Bill, 1997).

Chapter 12

Social relationships

"I've realised that if I say what I think, I'll have no friends left. But sometimes I just can't help it" (Raúl, 26 years old).

Social relationships, or rather, difficulties making them, tend to be one of the key signs of a potential autism diagnosis. There are in fact certain degrees of difficulty, with lack of interest in interaction being one of the fundamental criteria when it comes to making an autism diagnosis. As with so many other symptoms, it's just that: a sign that indicates that something more is going on and which needs to be explored before making an assumption as to the difficulties someone might face. We'll see how clinically speaking, this process is simplified in favour of convenience and we'll focus on the key signs that are generally used in order to intervene.

Generally, especially in autistic children, the significance of a lack of interest in interaction is normally mentioned. And, although it's a fundamental factor (it's the person's motivation that makes them communicate), disguising this symptom as a nuclear characteristic of autism remains dangerous. Many studies have shown that this lack of interest is a myth, right from the start. What really happens is that when the autistic child interacts with their surroundings they aren't seen as interactions, aren't detected, and therefore there's no reciprocity or encouragement from adults (Toth et al., 2007). The consequence of this is logical: if I use all the resources, I have access to and don't achieve it, I'll stop making an effort, because it's useless. On the other hand, within the clinical definitions of autism, qualitative alterations in interaction have always been mentioned, not their necessary absence (Albores et al., 2008).

The difficulties autistic people face in terms of adapting their behaviour to different contexts are often mentioned as being another key aspect of challenges in terms of interaction. As we've seen throughout this book, autistic people are logical, pragmatic and coherent. Many of the contextual adaptations society expects require continuous and fast adaptation. In general, most people on the spectrum feel as though they're 'hiding' their reality, likes/dislikes or preferences based on something without a specific protocol, which is something they find incredibly frustrating. And it's true: many of the social protocols are absolutely absurd, but neurotypical people make and follow them as they don't give them that much importance and can quickly adapt their behaviour according to the parallel analysis of many key aspects that occur in a specific context.

Both in autistic children and adults, the flow of a conversation can sometimes be complicated. Children struggle to follow certain rules when it comes to starting, maintaining and ending conversations. These rules, which they see as a 'waste of time', are key in terms of maintaining the conversation between neurotypical people. These are rules that are earned throughout their early years, through experiences with interaction and the generalisation of lessons learned in other contexts. As we know, these are both complicated for autistic children.

- *Give me that, I want to play.*
- *Shouldn't you say hello to me first?*
- *Why? You already know I'm here. And I'm not asking you for a favour, it's right next to you so you don't have to make any effort.*
- *But you always have to say please when you ask for things.*
- *But earlier you asked dad for something and you didn't say please.*
- *I was in a rush!*
- *Me too!*

The rules of social courtesy are a social construct, which is also permeable, changeable and, therefore, difficult both to internalise and generalise. It's possible that an autistic person doesn't understand their use other than a mandatory social norm. At the end of the day, isn't that just what they are? In order to try and generalise their use, the surroundings must be incredibly consistent and, on the other hand, we need to work on aspects related to mentalist skills so the child understands why this is important for others and how to use it as a communication tool in their favour.

As we get older, these rules and conventions become increasingly complex. Let's take reassuring phrases as an example. In the chapter on mood swings, we've already seen that a lot of what's expected of the other person depends on where they are on the emotion-pragmatism curve. In general, an autistic person has a quicker evolution than a neurotypical person, which together with certain protocols of action can lead them to be perplexed in certain contexts.

"I feel for you. I've never understood that phrase because I don't know what you're feeling. I thought it was a good thing that the person had died because they were suffering, but my husband told me not to say anything of the sort. I suppose they just want to say that they're sorry" (Águeda, 35 years old).

For adults on the spectrum who have generalised the use of social conventions (even if they've done so mechanically), the issue occurs when these are used in a non-literal way. For example, when a conversation is started with "How are you?", when the truth is they're not asking you "how you are". If we add in the fact that depending on each context and situation, the nuances can change, we're putting the autistic person in a truly defenceless situation.

-So, Daniel, when they ask "how are you?" at work, they're not really asking how I am?
- Exactly. They might just be saying hello.
- Might?
- Yes, because on certain occasions they may want to know how you are.
- May?

As we can see in this example, what I was trying to explain to the autistic person is that verbal communication depends significantly on so many things other than the literal message being transmitted, such as gestures, facial expression, type of eye contact, or speed and tone of voice. And, in addition to all that, the context in which the conversation takes place, the type of relationship you have with the other person and even the events that may have occurred in the minutes, hours or days prior to that interaction. So, what does this require? We saw this in chapter 5: a quick, superficial analysis of multiple information channel, information inference skills (mentalist) and a response adapted to the emotional state of the other person. That's it.

So, what happens when the message they transmit to us verbally or in writing doesn't correspond to the actual request? The following image is an example of this, where a person on the spectrum receives a WhatsApp message from their supervisor at work.

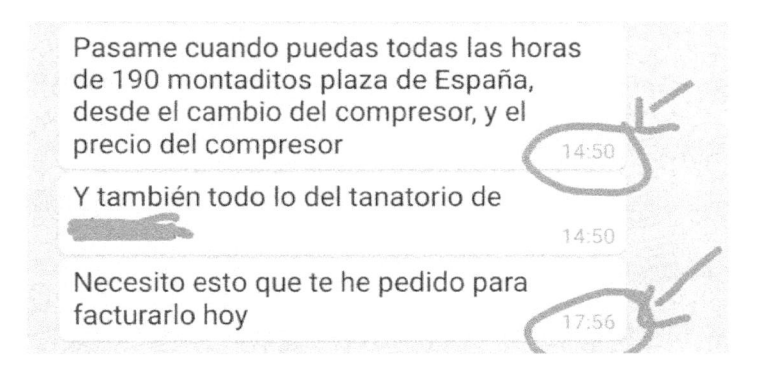

> Pasame cuando puedas todas las horas de 190 montaditos plaza de España, desde el cambio del compresor, y el precio del compresor   14:50
>
> Y también todo lo del tanatorio de ▓▓▓▓   14:50
>
> Necesito esto que te he pedido para facturarlo hoy   17:56

WhatsApp messages[79]. So, what's the deal?

A person might think that when someone says 'when you can', that's exactly what it means: do it when you've got the time or when you haven't got any other work. But the truth is, the majority of the time (emphasis on majority) in a work context, this expression indicates a rush, or absolute priority. We've delved straight into the realms of insinuation and formalities that occur in certain contexts and in which people on the spectrum are at a complete disadvantage. I mean, how can they not

---

[79] "When you can, send me all the hours for 190 Montaditos in Plaza de España, the compressor changes and the compressor price. And everything for the mortuary. I need all this so I can invoice it today"

me? Processing this ambiguous information requires parallel processing, adaptation to changeable contexts, absurd rules, unwritten protocols, processing the symbolic field and undertaking theory of mind. Wouldn't it be easier to just be clear and specific? Do neurotypical people think that interacting without this level of subterfuge is wrong? Well, it would appear so.

As both adults and children on the spectrum, you need specification and anticipation, and that's what you should ask of your surroundings: when you're given non-specific, incongruous or confusing information, tell them you need specific information. In work environments, invoking professionalism tends to be very effective. This is easier in certain sectors such as computing, as all of the work is undertaken following organisational techniques such as SCRUM[80], but even so, there can be certain exceptions.

One of the first aspects worked on with autistic children following their diagnosis is spatio-temporal structuring of their environment, which should also be done with adults. An autistic person needs an incredibly structured environment (or at least to start with), which is also linked to their relationships with other people, wherever possible and to the extent to which this specificity can be requested. A person's comfort is the cornerstone[81] to establishing good interaction.

An autistic person should be able to feel comfortable in their surroundings, information should be as specific as possible, without ploys and without double entendre: clear, direct and

---

[80] SCRUM is a working framework that has been visually structured in order to develop projects.
[81] Term often used to refer to something or someone who has played a very important role in order for an event or situation to take place.

sincere. Some people argue that communicating in this way implies rudeness, but as seen from an autistic perspective, we could say the same thing: is there anything more inadequate than giving a message that depends on the other person's interpretation? Isn't giving a message that leaves the other person in doubt, inadequate?

When we take this to the extreme, we're talking about using lies as a communication tool and to manipulate. It's common for this to occur in different contexts of social interaction and this can be difficult for autistic people to identify, due to the tremendous use of mentalist and symbolic skills it requires (Rivière, press). Sometimes, the flexibility of the neurotypical mind (which doesn't give anywhere near as much importance to the specificity of information) is also understood as a lie, to a certain extent, by some people on the spectrum.

"I really don't like being lied to. This includes people telling me we're going to one place and we end up going to two, or a different one" (Blanca, 36 years old).

Important: this doesn't mean that people on the spectrum don't know how to lie and cannot use this resource. In fact, many autistic people learn that using lies is a more socially-accepted strategy than being honest, and it's often used to avoid social commitments, for example.

Something similar occurs with the sense of justice, which is incredibly present in autistic people. Generally speaking, an autistic person sees what is true and what is false. There's neither a midpoint nor grey areas. Unfortunately, this world is built based on incongruences, totally unfair situations, half-truths and even socially recognised and accepted myths. Given that the world is full of incoherences, it's not unusual for autistic people, who don't conform to this reality, find it very frustrating that neurotypical people have a more permeable sense of reality (and justice). This strong sense of justice is particularly common among women on the spectrum, according to Tania Marshall (2014). This Australian psychologist even defines a type of autistic woman: "[…] obsessed with justice, equanimity and what is good and what is bad. This becomes an obsession, trying to organise groups that don't prosper because of their bad ways". The truth is, the cognitive constructions of a person on the spectrum tend to be dichotomous and, although it's true that this means their thinking is generally inflexible, isn't having a consistent and unchangeable opinion the key to being able to defend a cause?

In general, this very vehement expression of opinions isn't well received by neurotypical in most contexts. In fact, the autistic person's perspective tends to be censored for being 'inflexible' or 'categoric'. This way of processing is inherent for the person on the spectrum and often leads to them being invalidated, even their feelings, when they're likely just doing or saying what they believe in.

Similarly, an autistic person can encounter difficulties interacting with people who are discussing a topic on which they don't have a firmly constructed opinion, and therefore prefer to stay on the side-lines, without intervening (which can lead to other people feeling suspicious of them). This is the argument built upon ignorance: neurotypical people talk and give their opinion on absolutely everything, despite the fact the information they have regarding a specific topic is incredibly vague or even non-existent.

"We went to a party hosted by some of my partner's friends. I didn't realise at the time, but it turns out that I spent the entire time in the same

place, without moving. I spent the majority of the time alone, except when my partner came over to find out how I was and the odd person who tried to interact with me. I was like another piece of furniture" (Gustavo, 45 years old).

Group conversations are an absolute nightmare.

Group interactions can be particularly stressful for a person on the spectrum, as we've seen previously. Too many parallel signals, too much to analyse and too little time to do it in. The result tends to be the autistic person feeling 'trapped' in these sorts of interactions, and it's likely they stay silent, waiting for a way out. The image this lack of intervention by the autistic person creates in the minds of the other people in the group is yet another issue.

"A work colleague with whom I have a slightly closer relationship told me that the other employees thought I was weird, because I never said anything. I do actually want to interact, but sometimes they speak very fast,

interrupting all the time, and sometimes I'm not at all interested in what they have to say, so I just switch off" (Alba, 32 years old).

We've already seen that neurotypical people act based on the information they communicate via inference, using theory mind, while people on the spectrum act using certainty. What type of processing is more adequate? The truth is, none of them. They all have their advantages and disadvantages. But a society that prioritises effectiveness over efficacy (which works more or less well, although it has its faults) prioritises fast processing, although not based on absolute truths.

AUTISTIC	MORE INFORMATION	LESS INFERENCES	EFFICIENCY (+QUALITY −SPEED)	NEEDS MORE TIME
NEUROTYPICAL	LESS INFORMATION	MORE INFERENCES	EFFECTIVENESS (+SPEED −QUALITY)	NEEDS LESS TIME

Types of information and executions.

Tips

Much of the difficulties encountered when it comes to finding tools is the incredible variability of all the potential situations and contexts in which someone intervenes throughout their lifetime. Even so, I'm going to try and give a series of general guidelines.

Neurotypical people can be together, without a clear objective, just to 'hang out' or 'see what happens'. This lack of anticipation and objectives is not adapted to the way an autistic mind processes information. Both for children and for adults, all social interactions should have a clear objective and a time restriction. It's equally important to establish a clear beginning and end to the activity. This may appear simple, but it's one of the most effective in terms of global strategies.

For children, it's especially important to understand that multi-tasking should be avoided, as it can cause overwhelm. Interactions should be started one-by-one and should increase progressively. When it comes to games, these should start simple, each turn should be shown visually and shouldn't be particularly demanding of executive functions (at least at the beginning).

We're aware of the importance neurotypical people give to making eye contact with someone, as if this was the same as undivided attention. Many autistic people take this instruction literally (of course) and when they try and force eye contact, they do so very intensely and continuously, which the person they're looking at finds unnerving, unsurprisingly. There are different strategies you can use to make sure eye contact is less 'invasive' for the person you're looking at. In fact, it can normally be done semi-automatically, so that you don't lose sight of other signs, such as the verbal message during the conversation.

Pattern in the shape of an infinity sign when looking at a face.

Another relatively common aspect is confusing relationship circles, given that for neurotypical people relationships are both permeable and changeable. This isn't the case in autism, but at the same time, we can see how certain reactions can be seen as very categoric. "They're either my friend or my enemy" is quite common and understandable in black or white thinking.

"Now I think the key is that nobody ever taught me limits within relationships. My parents assumed I knew where the line was between a friend, best friend and a relationship with a partner. That couldn't be any farther from the truth. I don't know where the limits of trust are, I don't know what topics can be spoken about in one or the other, and I can end up in serious trouble, because it's a learning process that occurs over time,

and sometimes subconsciously for neurotypical people, but it isn't always that easy for autistic people" (Neurodivergente, on her blog).

I worked with this person to address these concepts through relationship circles (as I told you, it's a multipurpose tool) and, with this visual aid, her perspective on relationships changed: she learned that not all people have the same level of trust and that, in certain contexts, it's best to be wary when it comes to communicating certain things or personal information.

The topic of intimate relationships could be a book on its own accord, and it would be twice as thick as the one you're holding. A TV character, the psychiatrist Frasier Crane, defined the art of flirting as: "Relationships are like a tango[82]". Nick Dubin (2009) highlights: Dates are like a game and, unfortunately, many of us don't intuitively understand the rules". Many people on the spectrum have severe difficulties in all interactions related to romantic relationships. In these relationships, especially at the start, insinuations, duplicity and of course, the symbolic field, in addition to inference of desires and mental states by way of theory of mind and executive functions (plan, postpone, inhibit) play a decisive role.

"If they're interested in someone, they act like they're not interested at all, in a supposed attempt to get the person they're trying to win over to become interested in them. I don't understand why this would be, or at least for them, successful" (Águeda, 35 years old).

In a relationship, neurotypical people want their partner to sense their emotions. For them, it's a way of showing their partner's interest in them, anticipating their desires. And, on

---

[82] The tango is a type of dance in which two people dance very closely, moving forwards and backwards together. When it appears one movement is about to occur, sometimes the opposite happens.

the other hand, this supposes an ego defence mechanism if their (indirect) request is not fulfilled by their partner. All this forms part of the enhancement of the use of symbolic language (similes, jokes, metaphors…) in almost all social contexts, but especially when we relate to others on an emotional level. But, for someone on the spectrum, sensing these signs is sometimes very complex and insinuation-based communication, or directly 'lies', in search of the insistence of a partner is a genuinely difficult task.

"My marriage fell apart. According to my wife, I wasn't able to understand her. I remember she would get angry because when she would go somewhere I'd ask: "Do you want me to go with you?". She'd say: "No need", so I didn't do it. But when we saw each other again, she'd be angry and explained to me that she did in fact want me to go with her, but I had to instigate it. I don't understand it at all" (José, 56 years old).

Sexuality and gender identity is a topic barely discussed in relation to autism, but in general, studies appear to suggest that people on the spectrum tend to identify with a different gender identity to that which they were assigned at birth, or express their gender identity differently to neurotypical people. In general, this variabity tends to be observed more in women than in men. A study undertaken by George and Stokes (2017) showed that women on the spectrum have a greater tendency to be asexual, bisexual or homosexual than neurotypical women. Developing a different identity can be very sensitive and confusing and, in fact, it can cause yet another obstacle when it comes to an autistic person establishing significant relationships.

Sincerity is a value that fluctuates significant depending on context. This absolute sincerity, pragmatism and sense of reality and justice, often comes to work against people on the spectrum. On many occasions, neurotypical people prefer either for the truth to be hidden, or spun, because they find it harder and need time to digest it. The concept of the 'white lie'[83] is based specifically on this.

As they're so sincere at all times, autistic people can make social 'mistakes' such as sharing sensitive information or being too direct. The term 'inappropriate' or 'rash' tend to be quite common when certain neurotypical people refer to autistic people. When talking to an autistic person, they said:

-I tell my husband the truth and he thinks I'm being disrespectful to him and that I treat him like shit.
-How do you tell him? How do you say it?
- Is that important? Isn't what you say more important than how you say it?
- Sometimes it's the complete opposite...

The work we can do here to prevent these situations from occurring goes back to the analysis of the links that join us and those people, specifically. The closer these people are to our most intimate friendship circles, the freer we are to be ourselves. By analysing their mood (their ascending and descending curve, as we saw in chapter 8), we can either create a more direct message (pragmatic), or a more indirect focus (emotional support).

---

[83] A type of lie told so as to avoid someone getting hurt.

> **Crautista**
> @crautista
>
> Hoy una amiga ha tenido un problema y se siente muy mal. Ella es NT, así que gracias a tener mi diagnóstico, en vez de serle sincera e intentar buscar una solución, le he estado escuchando y dándole ánimos.
> Mañana si quiere quizá sí puedo buscar con ella una solución.
>
> 9:36 p. m. · 11 may. 2021 · Twitter for Android

Tweet[84] by @crautista. And they say that autistic people don't adapt.

A different processing system means a different understanding of both communication and social interaction. It couldn't be anything else, could it? People on the spectrum are sincere, resolutive, pragmatic and direct. This doesn't tend to cause losses of time, pointless conversations, hidden messages and duplicity in the delicate neurotypical world full of absurd protocols. Paradoxically, the direct messages communicated by autistic people tend to be misinterpreted by neurotypical people, who become overwhelmed by such sincerity and it doesn't fit in with their expectations. They end up giving hidden meanings to messages that are nothing but genuine descriptions of the autistic world about themselves and their surroundings. For a neurotypical person, 'getting straight to the point'[85] can be very inappropriate in certain contexts and they use a series of language resources to introduce a particular topic or ask a question or make a request. In fact, not doing this is consid-

---

[84] A friend had a problem today and feels really bad. She's NT, so thanks to my diagnosis, instead of being blunt with her and looking for a solution, I've listened and consoled her. If she wants to, maybe we can look for a solution together tomorrow.

[85] Non-literal expression used to refer to addressing the most important part of a specific topic.

ered a lack of empathy, as it doesn't adapt to the emotional state of the person in receipt of the message or question. In other words, there's an unwritten requirement to 'prepare the potential impact of the information'.

The real difficulty posed here is that, if as people on the spectrum you want to have a 'successful' conversation with neurotypical people, you need to make a conscious effort to pay attention to multiple signals, when your cognitive system isn't actually designed to do this. This is why you need to choose your battles carefully[86], because the price you pay for doing this continuously is incredibly high, as we'll see in the next two chapters.

---

[86] In this context, battles refer to "pushing oneself" or "making an effort".

Chapter 13

Anxiety and autism

"Anxiety has plagued me throughout my whole life. I actually thought it was a part of my personality. Now I know that I've been incredibly harsh on myself and I'm not the only guilty party, that being different doesn't make me useless, I just forced myself to do things because I thought that's what I was supposed to do: I could have avoided so many instances of head hitting, cuts and destructive thoughts" (Carlos, 52 years old).

It's incredibly common for people to mention a low frustration tolerance during an autism diagnosis process. It's still one of those sentences, let's not kid ourselves, that transforms an inherently negative characteristic into a limiting and incredibly unfair judgment, especially when we stop to think about the context within which this intolerance occurs.

As we've seen throughout this book, people on the spectrum are 'strangers in this world'. All autistic people, from children to adults, have to deal with the ups and downs of neurotypicals, while carrying the extra weight of having a different way of processing and perceiving reality: hypersensitivity, polarised thinking, the unpredictable nature of our surroundings, difficulty anticipating other peoples' thoughts, thinking literally....

These are aspects that outside of our world, in an alternative reality or perhaps an autistic utopia, may not only not be a hinderance, but may actually become an advantage. But today, they can be a nightmare due to the lack of adaptations within hostile and incredibly selfish surroundings that only work for the majority (neurotypical). It therefore comes as no surprise that autism and anxiety are, unfortunately, often linked.

Anxiety is the comorbid condition par excellence in an autism diagnosis. In fact, in late autism diagnoses it's common for the person to have been previously diagnosed with 'generalised anxiety'. Studies have demonstrated that even in situations of supposed rest, people on the spectrum have high levels of both cortisol and adrenalin compared to their neurotypical peers (Bitsika et al., 2015).

As you can imagine, the challenges faced by someone on the spectrum start early on, including frustration and consequently, anxiety. Some studies show that approximately 40% of minors with an autism diagnosis showed a comorbid anxiety disorder (Steensel et al., 2011). These studies tend to present forms of anxiety, as if highlighting them without understanding the underlying mechanisms and challenges was truly relevant. For me, the most important aspect is to discover the nature of the cause of the anxiety itself, given that one sole process produces different manifestations of anxiety, even for the same person.

The different forms of anxiety are intrinsically linked to the mechanisms of perception and information processing we've seen in this book, and that, together with interaction with the surroundings, create an imbalance which leads to anxiety in all its many guises. Generally speaking, all manifestations of anxiety may be linked to one of these general situations:

1) Sensory and information overwhelm: due to, on the one hand, excess stimulants and the impossible nature of their prioritisation and control of the amount of information processed at a high level. And, on the other hand, the imposition of processing a significant amount of information very quickly.

2) Unpredictability: lack of anticipation of events or occurrences that put executive functions to the test.

3) Anxiety related to social interaction: difficulty making inferences as regards the emotions and intentions of others, in addition to challenges when interpreting their own emotions.

4) Polarised thinking: difficulties creating responses that fit into a wider range of required possibilities and resorting to rigid and non-permeable patterns.

Before getting stuck straight into the consequences and manifestations of anxiety in autism, we need to discuss what happens prior to exceeding this tolerance, ultimately leading to anxiety.

We all have limited levels of physical and mental energy that help us undertake our daily tasks. These tasks can be more or less automatic, straightforward, or they may require more effort. Throughout the day, these energy levels fluctuate, decreasing as we undertake tasks and increasing as we eat or rest, and if we don't do this appropriately, even the simplest of tasks can become arduous.

Neurotypical people can do the majority of these tasks on 'autopilot', taking advantage of an operating system designed to do lots of things at once, quickly and superficially. They can easily deal with unexpected events, generating execution alternatives. Social interaction barely implies any mental exertion for them, in fact, it often helps them recharge this energy. On the other hand, from the moment they wake up, an autistic person has to fight against a world that moves too fast, forces them to process in parallel when their system is set up to process sequentially, and in which there's an often absurd amount of interaction, all of which depletes their energy levels.

"After work, my colleagues ask me to go for a drink with them. I just think, haven't you had enough interaction for the day? You haven't stopped talking since you got to work!" (Marc, 28 years old).

Once you've received your diagnosis, both in children and adults, one of the most important tasks is to get to know yourself as best you can so as to avoid this energy exertion having an impact beyond that which is evident. In children, it needn't be said that they need external support, as we'll see in the tips later in this chapter. For autistic adults, it starts by accepting that they're on the spectrum, the benefits of their condition and the challenges. The first step is to admit that 'you're not like the rest', at least not like the majority and, therefore, you can't compare the challenges they face with your own.

Going back to Marc, a computer programmer who often experienced lots of negative feelings about himself, as well as negative self-concept. Marc tried to fit in with his colleagues, which is why he forced himself to meet up with them after work. The result? Constant meltdowns and shutdowns, frequent trips to A&E and even admissions. When he was finally able to recognise he was autistic and neurodivergent, he understood that he didn't need to force himself to do certain things he didn't like, and he definitely didn't need to compare himself to people with significantly more social activity: "I've learned that it's a war I cannot win. But at the same time, in other situations I can be myself and really shine".

All autistic people should recognise their strengths, as well as the circumstances that don't favour their way of processing reality and analysing information. This is the best way to protect oneself from anxiety. To do this, they should monitor the energy we have available to us in terms of facing the day-to-day challenges posed by this unpredictable and hostile world.

If you're on the spectrum, you're probably familiar with Christine Miserandino's "spoon theory" (2003). Christine developed this theory as a way to explain the day-to-day challenges she faced as a person with lupus[87]. Each spoon represents a unit of energy, and each day began with a limited number of spoons. Christine had to carefully choose which tasks to complete, given that each task would require a certain number of spoons. In her case, this energy was physical energy, due to the nature of her illness. It was very important to choose which tasks to do, given that, for example, taking an evening shower could leave her without spoons to then have dinner.

Although Christine used the spoon metaphor to express her levels of physical energy, many people in the autistic community (and other forms of neurodivergence) have reworked the theory, and counting spoons has become their way of counting the ebbs and flows of their mental energy in terms of how they interact with the world. We often see social media messages such as "it uses up my spoons" or "sending you spoons" between people on the spectrum, referring to the energy con-

---

[87] Lupus is an auto-immune disease with varied symptomology, and it can be incredibly limiting.

sumed by social interaction or sensory overwhelm, and well wishes and expressions of solidarity.

Another relatively common way of calculating this energy and its use is to work in percentages (which, of course, is an estimation, just like spoons), similar to the remaining battery on a mobile phone. As a mobile phone is an essential part of our day-to-day life, I think this analogy is simple, especially when explaining the concept to younger autistic people. When talking to one of the young people I work with:

- *See? When you unplug your phone charger when you get up in the morning, it's on 100% power, just like you, if you've slept well. If not, you might be at about 80%, for example.*
- *So, when I use Google Maps, which zaps a lot of battery power, it's similar to when I do something I don't enjoy.*
- *Exactly! You need to be aware, but without becoming obsessive, and keep an eye on how your internal battery is doing. If you haven't got much power left at the end of the day, would you start playing Pokémon Go?*
- *No, because that takes a lot of battery…*
- *That's right, so maybe that day you should take a break from socialising and go home early.*

Perhaps unlike we may have thought, 'unintentional' activities aren't those that consume the most mental energy (or spoons). This is incredibly frustrating: the fact that it's an activity that the person on the spectrum wants to do isn't that relevant when it comes to the final consumption. For example, aspects related to parallel processing or amount of interaction pay a much more decisive role in the final energy consumption. If the autistic person is unaware of this circumstance, they may find themselves often confused.

"I was playing a game with my friends the other day. I'd been waiting for the event for ages and I had a great time playing for hours on end. But even though I ate and slept well, I was exhausted the next day and all I wanted to do was rest and not have to interact with anyone. It doesn't make any sense (Andrea, 26 years old).

Bill Nason (2011) proposed marking out a 'safe' zone that would be the equivalent of half of the daily spoons or 50% of the energy available. The idea behind it is to try and not go under this amount, so that if there's an event or events that require a significant amount of energy, we're not left totally drained, and can therefore avoid the consequences of this.

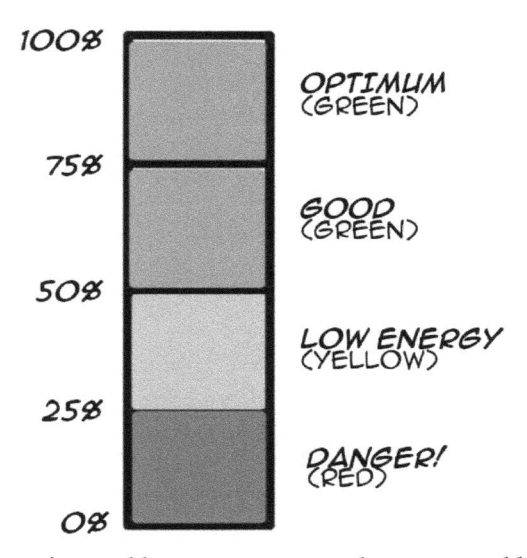

100% — OPTIMUM (GREEN)
75% — GOOD (GREEN)
50% — LOW ENERGY (YELLOW)
25% — DANGER! (RED)
0%

Look after your internal battery even more than you would your phone battery.

I remember when Hans, another autistic computer programmer, started to go through a phase where he experienced constant shutdowns and anxiety. He had been promoted at work and now, as well as working alone with his computer, he was responsible for a team. Hans' work was very good in both areas, but it wasn't long before the change started to take its toll. He started to pay the price for the continuous work meetings throughout the week. As he told me, it wasn't so much about the technical discussions during these meetings, but the moments where the conversation wasn't just about work, and other situations in which he wasn't sure how to respond quickly to a client requirement, which left him exhausted. He got to a point where his individual technical work started to become an issue, which really affected him because he's a perfectionist.

We began to analyse the situation and the solution was to spread the meetings out and always have a break between them. If he had a meeting on Monday, he'd try and make sure there wasn't another one until Wednesday. As his independent work was very much a hyperfocus, this enabled him to recharge the energy he used up during the meetings, so he spent a whole day on that after a meeting. This is how we managed to reduce the possibility of a meltdown and his anxiety levels reduced considerably.

Going back to the phone battery analogy, it's important for us to understand at which level of cognitive energy we're at when it comes to responding to the demands of our surroundings.

When we feel as though we're at 100% of our abilities, which tends to be at the start of the day, an autistic person feels full of energy and as though they're at full capacity, as long as they're well-rested. If this isn't the case, it's likely their mental energy is at about 75%, still in the green zone, but in a situation in which they might need slight support to undertake certain activities, which shouldn't be too demanding. When they get to 50%, they should start to be really alert: their energy level is at a point at which maybe they haven't got enough left to make it through to the end of the day: the yellow zone, and it's likely their top skills are compromised. At this point, the demands should be minimum, even when they're able to undertake sequential processes and hyperfocus. From 25% onwards, in the red zone, this is when the autistic person should be very careful as their energy level is borderline, and even the simplest of tasks can become impossible challenges, as well as being much more sensitive to sensory overload.

If we want to visualise it within the paradigm of spoon theory, we just need to do some simple conversions. 100% energy, the first green zone, is equal to having 'all the spoons'. In my experience, the less we divide these, the lower the chance of a meltdown. Let me explain: we can imagine that we have 100 spoons at the beginning of the day and they reduce gradually according to the events that occur. It's incredibly difficult to estimate how many spoons certain activities require, because they all have their nuances. However, if we base this on a smaller total, such as 8, it will be easier to assign how these are used in a way that doesn't use cognitive energy, and it's therefore much easier to anticipate without being left without spoons. If we start with a total of 8 spoons, equivalent to 100%, we'll have 6 spoons at 75%, 4 spoons at 50% and just 2 spoons at 25%

🥄🥄🥄🥄🥄🥄🥄 **OPTIMUM ENERGY**

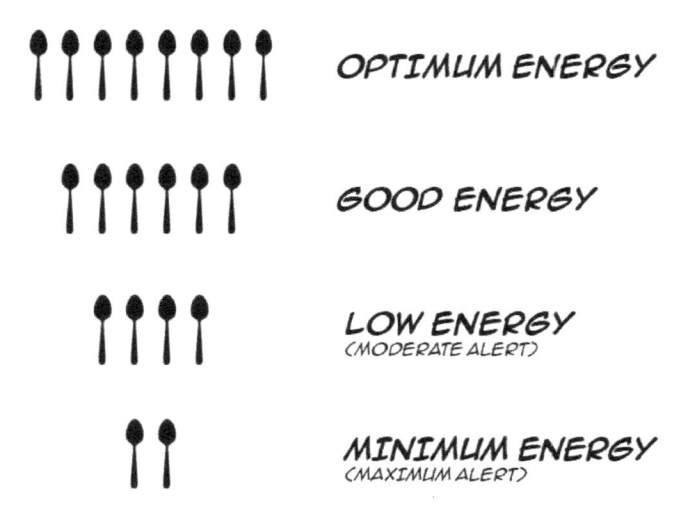

🥄🥄🥄🥄🥄 **GOOD ENERGY**

🥄🥄🥄🥄 **LOW ENERGY**
(MODERATE ALERT)

🥄🥄 **MINIMUM ENERGY**
(MAXIMUM ALERT)

Spoon theory applied to autism.

These visualisation systems aren't popular with all autistic people. One of the autistic people I work with uses a circular system, similar to a timer, because this makes the loss of energy compared to a total amount much more visible than with a system similar to the phone battery or loss of spoons. With one of the children, I work with I used the simile of Iron Man, one of the Marvel Comics characters he loves, and his armour. The armour has a limited energy level, and flying, lifting up objects and shooting uses energy. Just like Tony Stark[88], he should be aware of when he's running out of energy, so he isn't taken by surprise mid-air and end up crashing.

---

[88] Tony Stark is Iron Man's alter ego.

Even superheroes should be aware of their energy levels.

Each autistic person should choose the system that makes it easiest for them to foresee and calculate their cognitive energy. Important: try not to complicate this system too much. I've seen some autistic people with diagrams that even included equations and probability calculations. The only thing this achieved was giving them more anxiety and, on the other hand, they failed when it came to the basic objective of this system, which is anticipation. Whatever you use, it must be practical.

Not all events generate the same energy expenditure. Whether a system becomes more or less sustainable or, on the other hand, becomes an excessive hindrance or disorder, depends on many factors. This is why each tool should be personalised. However, and despite the variety of situations that provoke energy loss on the spectrum, there are groups of situations that will generate this loss regardless, with more or less impact. Some coincide with those that lead to anxiety, but this isn't always the case. As I mentioned previously, some activities the autistic person finds enjoyable can imply a tremendous energy expenditure. The type of events that lead to this energy expenditure is directly correlated with this 'faulty' interaction with the surroundings, and which I keep mentioning. However, this is the root of the majority of issues for autistic people:

1) Activities that involve processing various stimuli at the same time or undertaking parallel activities. For example, talking to a group of friends or family, or undertaking various important tasks at work at the same time.

2) Undertaking tasks or processes that are then subdivided into others, long-term tasks or without an established end. Or the generation or alternatives to a process that is generally undertaken in a different, specific way. Any type of unexpected event. For example, a trip that involves changes, or finding a different way of doing a work task.

3) Completing a displeasing task that requires an ambiguous or very permeable perspective, tolerating errors in their own execution or that of others. For example, putting up with the lack of precision in a given response when we require a specific piece of information, or not making a judgment on a circumstance we're incredibly sure of.

4) Tasks that require them to interpret the emotions of others. For example, judging other people based on their emotional state when they ask us for advice.

5) Assuming emotional states and meaning of external activities. Conversations with people we're not that close to or don't know, for example.

6) Making interpretations based on non-literal or ambiguous communication. For example, any information presented during a conversation and which we interpret incorrectly or don't fully understand.

7) Situations in which there's a sensory overload. For example, intermittent noises we cannot avoid hearing and cannot escape from.

8) In general, any situation that implies social interactions. Social meet ups, whether or not these are wanted, anticipated or unplanned.

9) A combination of any (or all) of the aforementioned situations.

As I'm sure you'll have realised, each of these groups of events corresponds directly to the chapters in this book, where I've described each of the main characteristics of the autistic idiosyncrasy. Number 1 corresponds to sequential processing, number 2 to executive functions, number 3 to dichotomous thinking, number 4 to mood swings, number 5 to theory of mind, number 6 to the symbolic field and lastly, number 7 corresponds to sensitivity and perception.

Each of these major groups of events can contain a very elevated series of situations that involve the way a person on the spectrum processes. This singular processing, together with the demands of the environment, may or may not lead to conflict. However, what is clear is that is produces energy expenditure.

In the following table, I've mentioned a series of situations that produce more or less energy consumption, according to the difficulty navigating hem poses. These situations vary between children and adults, but as you'll see, despite the fact that experience is included as a factor that could mitigate the impact and, therefore this energy consumption, there is a very clear pattern linked to the way an autistic person processes and therefore has a greater influence than acclimatisation or practice. Therefore, factors such as the amount of interaction (groups) or changes in general, are presented as practically immovable factors, regardless of how old the autistic person is.

	EASY	MODERATE	DIFFICULT	VERY DIFFICULT
CHILDREN	- BRUSH TEETH - GET DRESSED - FAVOURITE ACTIVITY	- PLAY WITH THEIR SIBLING OR FAMILY MEMBER - WALK TO SCHOOL - PLAY WITH A BALL	- PLAY WITH THEIR PEERS (NOT FAMILY) - DO THEIR HOMEWORK - GET A HAIRCUT - BATHE/WASH HAIR	- SCHOOL MEETING - PARTIES - LARGE GROUPS - LOUD OR INTERMITTENT NOISES - DENTIST/DOCTOR
ADULTS	-- AMILIAR ROUTINES - CONVERSATIONS WITH THEIR FAMILY - FAVOURITE ACTIVITY	- FAMILY GROUP CONVERSATION - GO TO NEW PLACES - GROUP ACTIVITIES	- GROUP CONVERSATION WITH STRANGERS - EXTERNAL JOBS - CHANGES - DOCTOR OR SIMILAR	- PARTIES - DATES - WORK MEETINGS
expenditure	10%	20%	30%	50%
	🥄	🥄🥄	🥄🥄🥄	🥄🥄🥄🥄

Energy expenditure for children and adults according to different events.

Meltdown

A meltdown occurs when the autistic brain is overwhelmed by excessive demands, whether sensory, social, cognitive or emotional. When an excess of information is produced very quickly and we don't give the brain time to collate the information, it collapses. Carolina, an autistic adult, says: "It's like when a computer freezes and the blue screen appears. That's how I feel".

In this situation, the brain cannot give adaptative solutions, nor can it create viable alternatives. It can only give basic 'fight or flight' responses. The 'fight' response could imply shouting, biting or hitting one's head. This response implies the brain focusing on a very clear and basic demand as a response to the event that has caused the meltdown, but it isn't in direct response to the event itself. During the process of a meltdown, the autistic person can lose control of their actions and these are therefore not intentional.

Nick Dubin (2009) highlights that, in essence, a meltdown is neither bad nor wrong. It's one of the body's natural responses:

> I see meltdowns as a similar bodily response to vomiting. Vomiting is neither good nor bad. It's just something that happens and it generally has a necessary function; something that hasn't agreed with you need to get rid of it. But vomiting isn't something you like doing in public, right?

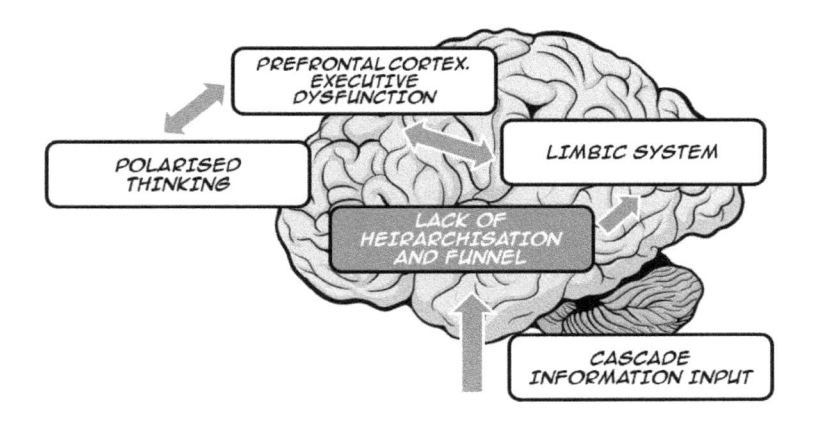

Cerebral process in an autistic meltdown.

Reconstructing the process at a sensory level, the cascade of information and the difficulties faced when putting said information in order of importance overwhelm the brain's limbic system, which is the focal point for emotional control, leading to panic. Despite the fact that the limbic system is constantly communicating with the prefrontal cortex, executive function found in autism prevents the cortex from being able to control the situation in order to generate a functional or more adaptive alternative. Dichotomous thinking doesn't help in these situations where solutions beyond 'all or nothing' seem miles away due to overwhelm. This leaves only one solution: the fight or flight response.

People on the spectrum can experience meltdowns on different levels: they can be physical, mental or emotional. Physically, an autistic person can lose partial or total control of their body. Sometimes they can even feel as though they're completely paralysed, similar to what occurs with sleep paralysis (incredibly frequent in autistic people, as we saw in chapter 11). On other occasions, this loss of control can have a completely opposite effect: the person can't stop moving, shouting or hitting out, which can be made worse if someone intervenes, or even worse, restrains them. The act of hitting, which is often considered pointless, actually redirects attention to the proprioceptive channel, allowing the overwhelm to be released, produced in a different part of the brain until balance can be restored. This is similar to what occurs in stimming, but more extreme.

On a cognitive level, a meltdown involves a momentary loss of control of higher brain functions. This is a very unpleasant experience. Who likes feeling as though they're losing control? The processes involved in impulse control, planning and attention are overwhelmed by the sensory system and emotional control centres.

"It's as though the rational part of my brain disappears for a few seconds. Afterwards, I feel incredibly guilty for having lost control" (Vanesa, 27 years old).

In these instances, trying to speak to the person who is in the middle of a meltdown can just make the situation worse, as you're requiring their brain to process even more information, when it's already overwhelmed.

The hostile environment that obliges autistic people to process in a way their system isn't designed for (as we've seen throughout this book) leaves their operating system constantly on the brink of collapse. In neurotypical culture, the incessant need to interact, the absurd nature of social conventions, imprecision and chaos non-autistic people get themselves involved in, autistic people constantly find themselves at a crossroads, with their stress and anticipatory anxiety levels always at a high and on alert as soon as they leave their safe spaces. This is why meltdowns tend to appear unjustified or an exaggerated response. In the case of adults, meltdowns are judged as a childlike and immature response to an event, in the eyes of a neurotypical person (but also those of an autistic person unaware of their reality), and totally insignificant.

But what actually causes a meltdown? As we've seen, there are two ways in which the overwhelm that leads to this reaction can manifest. This can be due to an accumulation of demands or sensory overwhelm, which is commonly known as 'the straw that breaks the camel's back', or an unpredictable event that is interpreted as a sudden change.

Burnout

Autistic burnout is the result of continued exposure to stress and anxiety. Some people on the spectrum consider burnout as a response to having to mask continuously (see the next chapter). However, some authors consider burnout to be a direct effect of executive dysfunction in autism; the deregulation of these functions in the frontal lobes would be the cause of the presence of this phenomenon in other conditions or disorders such as ADHD (Barkley, 1998 and Hinshaw, 2001).

In children, the consequences of burnout are those controlled by executive functions, such as the ability to concentrate, organise or even feel motivated. There's a clear decrease in activity as regards more day-to-day tasks. In adults, where the possibility of support is generally inferior to in children, burnout is normally expressed as an inability to undertake tasks, such as being unable to go to work or even engage in basic personal care. This tends to lead to forced isolation so as to avoid any form of social demand or interaction.

"I was fed up of trying to be normal. It just meant constant failure. I can't do everything that other people do, which makes me feel useless. The fact that they tell me how intelligent and able I am just makes me feel even worse. My only form of protection is to isolate myself" (Raúl, 32 years old).

Burnout is a slow-developing process that grows gradually throughout the first third of an autistic person's life. As a child, before they become aware of their differences (if they're lucky and this doesn't take until adulthood), they've already experienced some very destructive thoughts: I'm broken, incomplete and weird. They feel obliged to mask to fit in with their peers and feel accomplished, like other people. From adolescence onwards, stress turns into anxiety and starts to anticipate events where they know they're not going to have a good time. Slowly but surely (perhaps following their diagnosis), they'll start to create certain strategies, but the wide range of situations exceeds the protocols they've put in place and they inevitably end up failing. This type of learned helplessness where, whatever you do, you tend to end up losing, can break even the strongest will. So, following years of fighting, the person refuses to deal with more pain and ends up isolating themselves. Can we really blame them?

Shutdown

Shutdown in autism is often described in association with regressive behaviour. Its name implies what literally happens: the autistic person is experiencing exhaustion as a result of sensory overload, social demands or the combination of both, and simply 'shuts their system down'. In reality, their brain performs this operation as opposed to it being voluntary. Just as in a meltdown, shutdown appears and the autistic person cannot do anything, unless they've managed to anticipate it, of course.

Shutdown is predominantly expressed as isolation and inability to interact. During shutdown, it's common for the autistic person to lose the ability to communicate verbally (if they're verbal, of course), but they can communicate in part via other means. The person generally feels very attracted to calm environments, free of sensory stimuli, such as their bed, or sofa, for example. If they do anything, it's usually to do with their special interests, but even these can require more energy than they have at this point. Some people can spend weeks or even months in continuous shutdown, which to expert eyes can seem like depression.

"I could spend the whole day in bed. I didn't have the strength to do anything. Even going to the bathroom or talking to my children was a huge effort. Everything hurt me. I only found comfort curled up under a blanket" (Lorena, 42 years old).

They're not tantrums. It isn't depression nor stress.

So, are meltdowns, burnout and shutdowns inherent autism characteristics (or other forms of neurodivergence)? Or are they actually an exhausted cognitive system's response to having to force itself to perform beyond its limits, forced to undertake a task it isn't designed for? Wouldn't a neurotypical person collapse if their efforts to adapt were always unsuccessful, if the societal demands were constant and they were severely judged for any of their reactions to frustration.

Tips

As we've seen in shutdowns, it's easy to confuse them with more socially recognisable phenomena such as depression. That's why, before designing strategies that allow us to help both autistic kids and autistic adults, we must distinguish between them.

When it comes to meltdowns, the following are common:

A) In children they're often confused with tantrums and, if we act as we would if this were the case, this would make the situation worse, unsurprisingly.

B) Adults are judged more severely, involving suggestions of loss of control or voluntary behavioural manipulation.

So, how can we tell a childish tantrum from a meltdown? The following table highlights the main differential characteristics in each case. Generally speaking, a meltdown is characterised by the lack of willpower and control by the person who is experiencing the meltdown. When it comes to tantrums, even if they're superficial, the person who is having the tantrum does have a certain level of control.

TANTRUMS	MELTDOWNS
- CERTAIN CONTROL OVER THE SITUATION	- NO CONTROL OVER THE SITUATION
- THEY WANT TO GET SOMETHING OR GET OUT OF A SITUATION	- LOOKS LIKE A PANIC ATTACK OR INTENSE FEAR RESPONSE
- ENDS SUDDENLY IF THEY GET WHAT THEY WANT	- TRIES TO ESCAPE, REGARDLESS OF THE OTHER PEOPLE
- OBSERVES THE EMOTIONAL REACTIONS OF OTHER PEOPLE	- NO CLEAR DEMAND OR APPARENT REASON
- CAN TALK AND NEGOTIATE	- CANNOT CONVERSE
- IF THERE'S ANY AGGRESSIVE BEHAVIOUR, IT'S AIMED AT GETTING WHAT THEY WANT (FOLLOWING THE ADULT, FOR EXAMPLE)	- IF THEY HIT OTHER PEOPLE, IT IS AN ATTEMPT TO INTERACT OR CLOSENESS, IT IS NOT INTENTIONAL
	- SHOWS REMORSE

The difference between tantrums and meltdowns.

When it comes to a meltdown, there are two possible courses of action: prevention and support. The first refers to circumstances and actions we can do to avoid a meltdown from happening, which should definitely be the ongoing focus of our efforts. The latter refers to actions we should take if we haven't been able to prevent the meltdown, in order to minimise the potential effects.

In children, this effort should be made by adults. We should follow a series of instructions that are inevitable in terms of acknowledging the difference in processing as a fundamental principle. Once the adult understands, processes and assimilates that this child has a different way of functioning, everything else is so much easier. This series of principles are aimed at children, but they can simply be extrapolated and adapted for adults on the spectrum, too.

1) Different processing system: this includes sensory processing differences, different symbolic ability, difficulties recognising hidden social cues, etc.

   The expectations parents have of their children should be adapted to these processes, else, in addition to the surroundings, you'll put pressure on the child in their safe space, which is at home with their family.

2) Monitor their activities and take a guess as to their cognitive energy levels, as we've seen in this chapter: it's hard for adults to estimate this, so imagine how complicated it must be for kids.

   Give them time for rest and recovery, even if they don't appear tired. Remember: it's always best to anticipate than having to take action.

   The following graph is taken from the *The Autism Discussion Page: On stress, anxiety, shutdowns and meltdowns (2011)* by Bill Nason, and gives you an idea of the importance of these moments of disconnection from all demands.

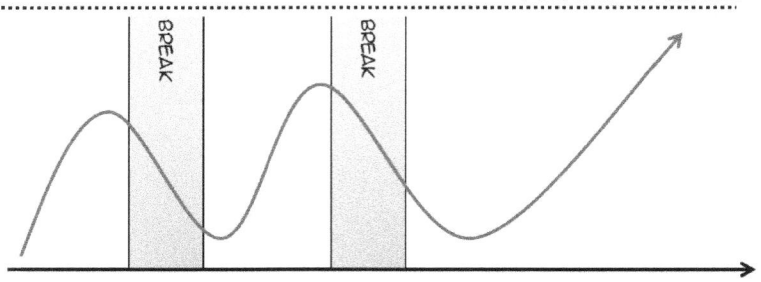

BUS/CHANGES/HISTORY/MATHS/CHANGES/LUNCH/CHANGES/GYM

Taking breaks throughout the day can help us prevent a meltdown.

3) Always give them space and time to develop their own methods of regulation, whether that be stimming, echolalia or others. This is their main tool for regulating their emotions.

4) Make a list of continuous triggers that you know can lead to meltdowns. Behaviour diaries are one of the key tools that we use as cognitive-behavioural psychologists, for one simple reason: they work. Written monitoring reveals many keys that go unnoticed if they aren't registered systematically. For example, going back and writing down the dream you just had. If you don't do it straight away, you'll probably completely forget about it.

But don't let your guard down. If a stimulus stops being a trigger, don't trust it. In this case, it could have been caused by many circumstances. Similarly, identify the physical stress signs that could lead to a meltdown, such as an increase in heart rate, sweating, etc.

5) In potentially stressful situations: anticipation. Always explain to autistic children what's happening, and adapt it to their level of understanding, with accompanying visual aids.

6) Always have a relaxation tool to hand, as this can help to increase the regulating impact of stims, if they aren't enough in this instance. Some autistic adults have a series of fidget toys that help reduce their stress, such as fidget spinners, etc.

In the long run, sports activities are also recommended, for more reasons than just their benefits for physical and mental health. In autism, the issue in terms of really getting into these activities is that they don't see immediate benefits if the person doesn't enjoy them.

How not to motivate an autistic person.

But, no matter how hard we try, meltdowns are inevitable and it's crucial we know how to act when they do occur. Whether you've got a family member on the spectrum or you're autistic and want to know how to properly deal with your meltdowns, here are a series of basic pointers.

Some authors such as Brenda Smith Myles (2005) like defining several stages within the course of a meltdown. I think this description is quite useful, as the strategies we can follow vary depending on which stage of a meltdown you're in. The author coins the first stage the 'rumbling state, in which the autistic person has a meltdown brewing, let's say. As we've seen throughout this chapter, and the book in general, an autistic person, especially if we're talking about a child, may not be fully aware of the fact that a meltdown could potentially occur. In my experience, this is predominantly due to interoception, lack of generalisation of learning, unawareness of triggers and sensory activation.

Each individual experiences this first stage differently. Some children start to lose the ability to speak, whereas others suddenly become hyperverbal. Some adults feel a prickling sensation on their skin or scalp, and others suddenly find themselves unable to concentrate. Some people describe it 'as if their brain starts spinning, gradually getting faster and faster'.

Regardless of how it manifests, if we manage to identify it (the register!), this is the time to act straight away, as later on it will be too late and our support will only be limited. If you're in an environment full of stimuli and too many demands, if you can, the best thing to do is to get out of there. In children, of course, we need to let them know we're going to move. If you can't completely leave the area, try to limit the amount of activity you or the child does. This is fundamental for people of all ages. You need to reduce the number of things you're doing (think back to slow, sequential processing). Use the regulatory tools such as stimming or objects (always carry them with you). Reduce the speed at which you're talking and what we ask of your child, and give them longer than you ordinarily would to respond.

If you haven't been able to catch the signs right at the initial stage, nor have you been able to put these strategies into practice or they haven't worked as expected, it's likely the autistic person goes into a meltdown, the 'rage state'.

Here, our support needs to be less direct, as any form of contact, even verbal, can have the opposite effect to what we were hoping for, thus increasing the intensity of the meltdown. The idea is to stay close to the person, but without interacting with them directly. You should focus on controlling their surroundings.

To start with, and although it seems obvious, you need to stop doing what you were doing, no matter how important it may be. Get rid of anyone nearby, both adults and children. Try and reduce all the variables that could increase the pressure on the sensory system as much as possible: turn off any sources of light and sound. The voice of whoever is trying to support the person should be quiet and calm, and should never be emotionally impacted by the intensity of the person who is having a meltdown. During this stage, you must not invalidate the autistic person, but just calmly let them know you're there. If possible, don't touch the person. Although that seems hard, sometimes it's better to let them hit their head than to grab hold of them and stop them.

STAGES OF A MELTDOWN

- INTEROCEPTION DIFFICULTIES
- LACK OF GENERALISATION
- TRIGGERS
- AROUSAL

RUMBLING STATE ↓ DIRECT INTERVENTION

RAGE STATE ↓ INDIRECT INTERVENTION

RECOVERY STAGE ↓ INTERVENTION UPON REQUEST

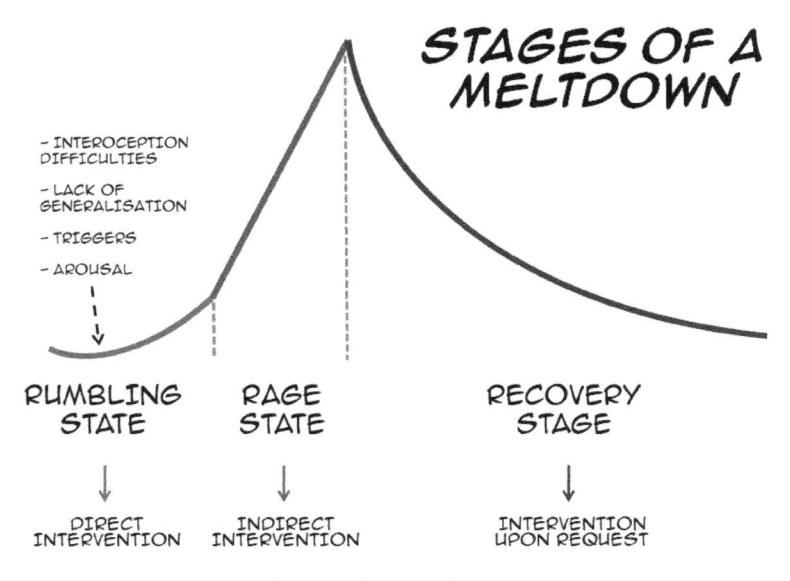

Stages of a meltdown.

I remember when Javier, one of the children I was working with, had a meltdown on a day trip. Javier became overwhelmed and unfortunately, I didn't know what signs to look for in him. He started to shout and squeeze his head, trying to stop the sensory overwhelm he was suffering from, and he also started to hit himself. Calmly, and without touching him (leading him with my body), I took him to a side street without any people around. In a calm voice I said to him: "Javi, I'm here. Don't worry, I'm not going anywhere". Slowly but surely, and keeping an eye on his reaction, I got closer to him so he could feel my physical presence, without forcing it. The pressure he was putting on his ears and the way he was hitting himself started to reduce and I began to see him try to get closer to me with his gestures. In the end, I was able to touch him, while telling him "It's going away, don't worry". I swapped the way he was hitting his head for soft, rhythmic patterns on his chest, following the movement he needed.

Occasionally, in other contexts such as at home, we can try and offer an alternative for the person experiencing a meltdown. Some children and adults on the spectrum find that following a series of movements or exercises actually substitutes their meltdown, almost as if it were an escape route for the dreadful discharge of energy. Either way, my experience tells me that when it comes to stimming, offering alternatives can help because it has a very similar form of physical expression to the actual meltdown. In people who feel the need to hit (themselves) during a meltdown, giving them a substitute such as a rubber hammer, pillow or similar can be helpful. I used to work with an autistic person who would break things by throwing them on the floor in the midst of a meltdown, so we found that using medicine balls was a good, less-dangerous substitute to throwing any objects within their reach.

During the last stage of a meltdown, the recovery stage, support from the people around them is crucial. Generally, children tend to feel confused, exhausted or even scared during this stage. An adult tends to feel embarrassment and guilt. Regardless of their age, it's still a moment of danger, as even though the 'anger' has gone, it can come back if we're not carefully; giving the person time and space is fundamental here. The intensity of the support and contact depends on each autistic person. The person giving this support should stay close and let them know they're there, without overwhelming them, but the most important thing is to not blame them.

All family and other people who interact with the autistic person should be aware of how to act before, during and after. At the special education centre in Badajoz, we had a protocol for each autistic person at the centre. These were extensive and created alongside their families.

Similar to a diabetic person with whom we should follow a specific protocol that could save their life, knowing how to act appropriately in the event of an autistic meltdown should be mastered by all health workers, security and other public sector employees. Unfortunately, even today there are still stories of autistic people who have died due to someone acting incorrectly during an autistic meltdown.

A shutdown is something along the lines of a final warning; the autistic person's cognitive system's final warning to say that "something isn't right, I've had to shut you down before irreparable damage is caused". If you experience a shutdown, listen to your brain: rest. This is the moment in which to stop and recharge. Going back to the mobile phone battery, this would be the equivalent of your battery being totally empty and, even if you plug your phone charger in, it takes a few minutes for it to turn back on again and show the battery at 0%. You've overdone it, so you need to stop and get your strength back.

Once you're somewhat reenergised, think about what has happened and how you ended up there, from a constructive and learning-focused perspective. Start slowly, following familiar routines that don't require a significant amount of energy, and little by little you'll start to return to normality. The fact that you've suffered a shutdown means that there are a series of circumstances that are draining you constantly. This isn't just due to a one-off event that may not happen again. There's something that's consuming a significant amount of energy. Stop and go over your routine, events and be aware of everything that may throw you off: it might be impacting you more than you thought.

If you're a family member of someone in shutdown, the basic requirements are similar to those of a meltdown. The first stage is to accept and adapt to the difference in processing and, therefore, their needs. Don't minimise their impact nor blame the autistic person, of course. Respect their silence and isolation and tell them you're available, but only once a day. Give them all the time they need to recover: only the autistic person can establish how long this takes, not you.

Chapter 14

Masking

"Masking is speciality. I wish that wasn't the case, because I'm very aware of how it affects my mental health and overall wellbeing, but there's not much I can do about that. I'm slowly but surely learning to unmask, but it's a long and complicated journey" (Jai, 27 years old).

Autism as a disorder that mainly affected males is pretty much common knowledge throughout the history of this condition. In fact, women make up just 20-25% (or 1 in 4) all autism diagnoses, a percentage that includes the total number of girls diagnosed with Rett syndrome, a very limiting disorder, as we saw in chapter 4. As a result of this, it was also affirmed that it had a greater effect on females compared with the average among males.

It's now recognised that there are lots of women on the spectrum, beyond Rett syndrome (which, in fact, isn't actually classified within ASD diagnoses). There are also professionals and environments within autism that resist moving on from the belief that there is a disproportionate number of cases compared to men, and maintaining this belief has more repercussions than you may think. To start with, if we continue to think of females as a minority on the spectrum, the diagnostic and intervention tools will continue to be focused on males. It's like the market law: we work for the majority of clients, not for the minority. We've already seen that early detection tools such as the ADOS-2 and ADI-R (the most-used and internationally standardised) may be ineffective in terms of identifying autism in women. On the other hand, and perhaps even more important, the erroneous calculation of 1 in every 4 definitely didn't help professionals who, when in doubt in certain cases, perhaps decided to rule out diagnosis in women. Statistics are a powerful pressure measure when it comes to making decisions (Halladay et al., 2015; Young et al., 2018). School reports aren't much help either, where when it comes to girls (who may come to receive an autism diagnosis at a later stage), teachers tend to say that they show more interest in interacting with their peers than their male counterparts (Sedgewick et al., 2016). Taking this measure as a fundamental sign of autism therefore often leads to their diagnosis being ruled out, too.

But despite the reluctance of some clinical environments, today we at least know that there are as many autistic women as there are men, if not more. In my case, over the last two years the women I've diagnosed have made up 73% of the total diagnoses I've made. Of course, I'm not saying this is the case for other professionals who diagnose around the world, but what's clear is that the trend in all professionals is to at least equalise the proportion. As a minimum, and according to some studies (Ruggieri, 2016), it's clear that "[…] women with ASD are underreported, especially those with a high cognitive performance".

For years, I've tried to emphasise that the detection of autism in women is very different from its detection in men, for many reasons:

1) In males, symptoms tend to be more externalised, and therefore it tends to manifest as hyperactivity and behavioural conditions. In contrast, symptoms in women are more internalised (depression, anxiety, somatisation and even eating disorders). This means that it's more visible in males, whereas in women it appears more subtle for much longer (if they're ever diagnosed).

   In accordance with some studies by specialists as regards the diagnosis of ASD, almost 70% of professionals indicated that women showed different autism symptoms to men. 54% also stated differences in comorbid conditions, with sensory and emotional issues among the most common (Jamison et al. 2017).

2) The dreadful gender bias. If a young boy doesn't play with other children, or doesn't communicate as expected for his age, alarm bells start to ring immediately and the professionals are brought in. However, if a young girl doesn't play with her peers and encounters communication difficulties, this is usually said to be because she's an 'introvert', 'shy', etc. Basically, it's seen as something normal because of her gender.

   In accordance with Ratto et al (2018), parental expectations in terms of social skills are key when it comes to how late many women receive their diagnosis. The majority of parental concerns tend to be linked to language (males and females) and social interaction (only in males) (González et al., 2019).

3) Some idiosyncratically 'historical' patterns such as recurrent interests are different in males and females.

Some studies conclude that in females, these interests or repetitive behaviours tend to be more functional than in their male counterparts (Hiller et al., 2014).

4) As regards frustration when it comes to interacting with their surroundings, women tend to feel guilty about their lack of effectiveness in interactions. Men, however, experience this differently. There's not such a significant feeling of guilt as can be identified in women and they express their frustration externally. In general, women adapt better to hostile environments (at least initially) and they're both more observant and patient. Men become frustrated more quickly and externalise this. They're less tolerant. Women try to understand it and get involved, which is where masking comes into play.

5) Tools: as I've already mentioned, these are designed specifically based on samples consisting predominantly of males. Since the work of the likes of Leo Kanner and Hans Asperger, the predominance of males over females in research samples has been clear (Kanner, 1943: Ruggieri & Arberas, 2016). This had led to a significant degree of masculine gender bias and a lack of sensitivity towards the female phenotype in diagnostic criteria and tools, due to their construction and validation with predominantly male populations (Lai et al., 2015; Øien et al., 2018).

6) And, finally, we must mention that the current diagnostic criteria (DSM, CIE) do not include a gender perspective. Not to mention that there are very few studies that have researched the relation between the early

ASD assessments and gender (Sipes et al., 2011). However, other research concludes that there are no differences between boys and girls with ASD in terms of their nuclear symptomatology (Worley and Matson, 2011).

So, what's masking and what differentiates it from imitative behaviours that can be observed in the overall population? First, we need to establish that masking is only one of the various parts of a more complex process known as camouflaging. Camouflaging is a series of strategies developed before, during and after social interactions. The purpose is to compensate for a supposed lack of skills, not exclusively social, and to hide autistic characteristics that are not socially accepted.

In general, as we've established, autistic women are more conscious of how they differ from other people than men are. In addition to a feeling of guilt due to not fitting in when it comes to social challenges, they establish a series of proactive strategies, whereas men tend to be more confrontational with their environment. They observe the surroundings, the behaviour of other people and try to imitate it, as it's clear to them that these behaviours are accepted by the people around them.

> Whether for constitutional reasons or social permeation, as autistic girls and women we actively aim to participate in the social world, and as part of that search we develop what is technically known as masking from childhood, which consists of a series of compensatory masking strategies that help us respond to what is expected of us: to appear normal" (Carmen Molina, CEPAMA, 2020).

According to the study by Baron-Cohen and collaborators (2019), this masking process consists of three different stages:

1) The first stage, known as compensation, and the autistic person aims to do just that: compensate for a series of social skills they don't have, consider inadequate or believe they don't have.

    - Copying the body language and expressions of others, including tone of voice and other communication resources.
    - Practicing these imitated expressions in safe spaces before putting them into practice.
    - Learning social skills and rules by watching TV series, films and reading books, and trying to explicitly understand the social norms via a list of 'rules'.
    - Using pre-prepared scripts based on these rules.

2) The second phase of masking is the masking itself. In this phase, the autistic person 'acts' out what they learned during the compensation phase, in social contexts.

    - Social situations generally tend to be a source of tension, so they control their expressions and body movements in order to appear relaxed.
    - Making forced eye contact.
    - They continuously control their 'performance' and the impression they're giving to others.

3) The third phase is assimilation. This phase consists of the autistic person justifying their performance, predominantly due to the social pressures of interacting

and the need to fit in in social situations. They therefore:

- Feel that making conversation with others isn't natural.
- Avoid interaction as much as possible in social contexts. On other occasions, due to the loss it could cause, or social pressure, they force themselves to interact. They're therefore permanently in this dichotomy.
- If they end up in social situations, they try to go unnoticed.
- They're not themselves: they're acting.
- They need the support of others in order to socialise.

Ultimately, the complete autistic camouflaging process aims to hide the autistic characteristics that don't appear to be socially accepted and which set off alarm bells for others (stimming, lack of social interaction, lack of eye contact and variety in non-verbal communication, recurrent conversations about a topic) and replace them with other behaviours that, having observed different environments (real and fictional), appear more successful ('adequate' bodily movements, significant social interaction, eye contact, multiple examples of non-verbal communications, small talk).

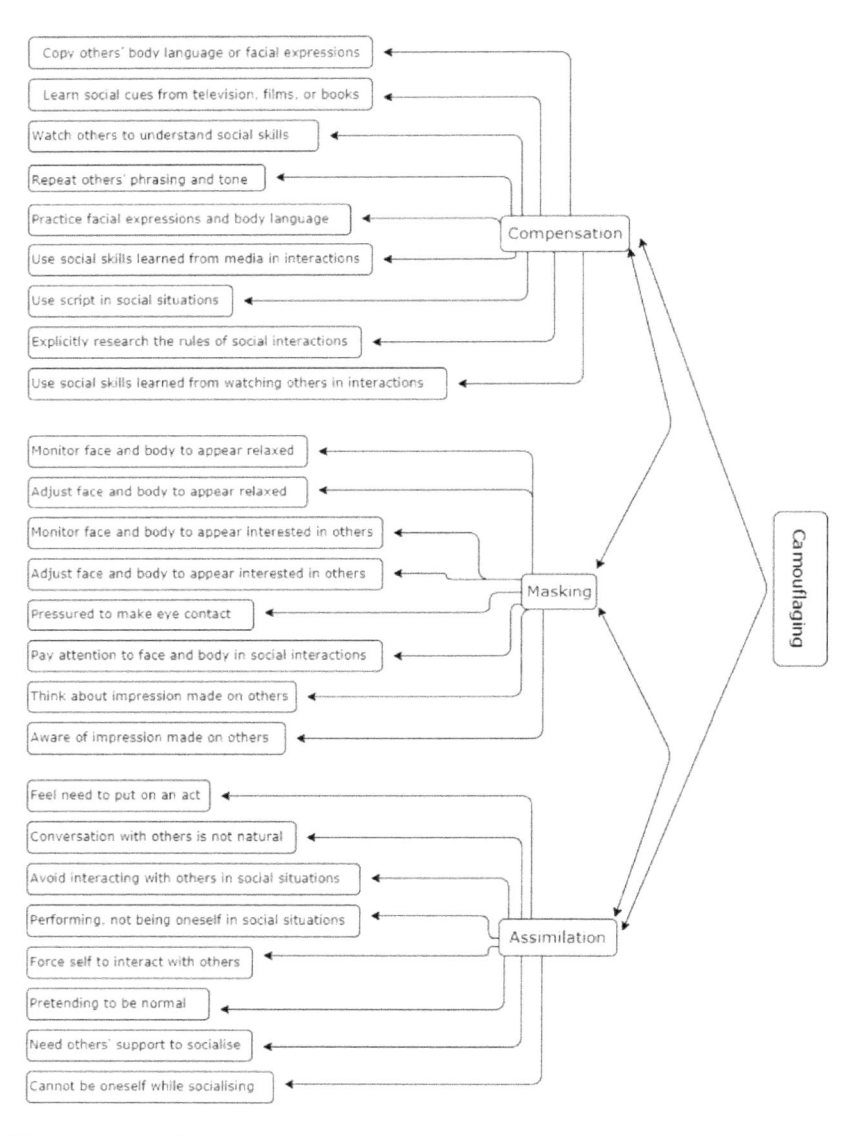

Compensation
- Copy others' body language or facial expressions
- Learn social cues from television, films, or books
- Watch others to understand social skills
- Repeat others' phrasing and tone
- Practice facial expressions and body language
- Use social skills learned from media in interactions
- Use script in social situations
- Explicitly research the rules of social interactions
- Use social skills learned from watching others in interactions

Masking
- Monitor face and body to appear relaxed
- Adjust face and body to appear relaxed
- Monitor face and body to appear interested in others
- Adjust face and body to appear interested in others
- Pressured to make eye contact
- Pay attention to face and body in social interactions
- Think about impression made on others
- Aware of impression made on others

Assimilation
- Feel need to put on an act
- Conversation with others is not natural
- Avoid interacting with others in social situations
- Performing, not being oneself in social situations
- Force self to interact with others
- Pretending to be normal
- Need others' support to socialise
- Cannot be oneself while socialising

→ **Camouflaging**

The camouflaging process, beyond masking (Baron-Cohen et al. 2019).

"I'd spend days collecting information from TV, films... and then I'd put it into practice. But it was never totally successful, because I always felt as though I was quite robotic, or something like that" (María, 27 years old).

As we've seen throughout the different phases of camouflaging, the processes of imitation are a key in masking behaviours. But what happens to make these imitation processes so 'robotic' and prevent them from being more natural in people on the spectrum? Could it perhaps be because the processes they want to undertake are not automatic behaviours in autistic people? Of course, that's exactly what it is. As they don't have socially accepted interaction strategies in their repertoire, the autistic person creates others that fill in the gaps, and they do so by imitating patters they observe in others, as well as studying what they read or watch in TV programmes, films, etc. (Baldwin and Costley, 2015).

The key difference between autistic and neurotypical imitation is that it's very rigid in autistic people, creating a very inflexible prototype. This makes it very difficult to transfer this to other situations, so their imitative pattern often doesn't work correctly, without mentioning that it doesn't feel like their own behaviour (unless masking is taken to an extreme, as I'll explain later on). Conversely, imitation processes in neurotypical people are spontaneous, from the early stages of development: they observe a behaviour and create a flexible behavioural prototype that can vary quickly, depending on the variables that arise in each specific context. These processes come to form part of natural behavioural patterns that are employed in different circumstances and events.

No, it doesn't work.

The processing differences in autism, in addition to mentalist skills, patterns of emotional recognition and the lack of adaptation to kids on the spectrum when it comes to involving them in activities that enhance their observation of others in natural contexts, explains, but only in part, the development of inflexible and minimally generalised behaviours that lead to camouflaging. What happens to all those girls we know start to mask from a very young age? Currently, masking detection tools are incredibly limited, with the exception of the CAT-Q Questionnaire (Baron-Cohen et al., 2019), which you can find at the end of this book, the ASSQ-GIRLS (Ormond et al., 2017) and the Questionnaire for Autism Spectrum Conditions Q-ASC (Attwood et al., 2011) are designed for adults. According to Sven Bötle (2019): "It's a shame that there's no version of this tool for children, as social camouflaging could lead to late diagnosis in women".

As I mentioned previously, the need to fit in socially and the feelings of guilt associated with this and the better observation and imitation skills lead to the percentage of women who mask being higher than the percentage of men (Kirkovski et al, 2013). This doesn't mean that this process doesn't occur in men, although the study undertaken by Baron-Cohen and his collaborators is pretty resounding in this sense. In this study, no differences in terms of camouflaging were found between neurotypical women and men, nor among non-binary people, although the sample used in these cases is very limited.

Masking behaviours start at different ages, depending on each individual autistic person. However, the cause tends to be their awareness of difference and loneliness. If a young autistic girl feels this way, it can only lead to negative consequences. Adopting a form of behaviour that desperately goes in search of social validation can lead to situations of both risk and vulnerability. There are significant numbers of cases of autistic women who are victims of gender-based violence and all types of family-based violence are abundant in cases of clinical diagnosis. On the other hand, the use of alcohol and drugs to make certain social contexts easier is common among young people. It becomes an issue when it becomes a requirement in order to engage in social interaction.

"I started with alcohol. I realised it help me let myself go and my weirdness (which I now know were because I'm autistic) went unnoticed because I was drunk and were therefore socially accepted. I then felt the need to be in that state all day, because when I was drunk, they were acceptable, but it I was sober they gave me weird looks because of how I spoke or moved. Because alcohol is looked down upon depending on the time of day, I switched to other substances that didn't make it so obvious that I'd taken them" (Sonia, 41 years old).

Many women learn to recognise their masking behaviours either during the diagnostic process or following their autism diagnosis. This is such a revelation for them: for so many years they've been playing a role in order to fit in socially, which has led to absolute exhaustion on so many levels. In many cases, this masking is so intense that they don't know where it ends and where their true self begins. In many cases, people come to realise that they don't know what they want to be like or how they want to behave naturally in basic situations such as being affectionate. In other cases, this mask is so deeply interiorised that they end up experiencing depersonalisation. In some of these cases, and in autistic people with prosopagnosia, the person can even be unable to recognise themselves in a mirror, not recognise their voice, handwriting or their gestures, due to the intense nature of the camouflage they have developed. Many women who have received their autism diagnosis in adulthood were given different diagnoses previously, such as Borderline Personality Disorder (BPD) or Dissociative Identity Disorder.

"I suffered with anxiety and throughout my school years. All specialists I saw focused on that instead of considering a potential autism diagnosis. At one point they even thought I had Borderline Personality Disorder (BPD) and I've suffered several admissions. There's definitely a gender bias, or at least there was in my case. Today, psychiatrists still question my autism diagnosis" (Cristina, 21 years old).

Another consequence of continuous masking is partial memory loss. Establishing a defence strategy such as camouflaging in order to partake in certain contexts and social situations involves playing a role or adopting a parallel personality. Many autistic people describe masking as being like being part of a theatre performance. Doing it for such a long time, even in their own home, becomes automatic. This means that they don't choose to mask, instead it kicks in automatically, making camouflaging subconscious. As this is the case, they become less conscious of their actions and their memory loss or lapse can be anywhere from minutes to even hours. This has clear cognitive and emotional consequences, even leading to feelings of depersonalisation because they cannot remember events, performances or even feelings.

"I thought I was going mad. I couldn't remember many of the things that had happened throughout the day. Now, because I'm aware of masking, I've realised that these were the situations in which I didn't allow myself to be me. Since masking less, these lapses are decreasing, and now I barely ever suffer memory loss" (Ana, 42 years old).

Tips

Masking poses significant risk to someone who is unaware they're autistic. Therefore, the first step is to embrace your diagnosis as something that defines you: your way of being, feeling and perceiving. Diagnosis plays a fundamental role in getting rid of feelings of guilt and shame. Continuously hiding behind a mask in social contexts is due to not feeling comfortable with who you are or your skills and you're carrying the weight[89] of the entire process of change and adaptation you think you're required to undertake.

As in all interventions with autistic adults, the use of tools on certain occasions is to be considered. In any case, this is what masking should be: just another tool. But the use of this tool should come with awareness of when and how much it's being used, as otherwise, instead of being a support mechanism it will become a hinderance.

"Following my diagnosis, my partner told me I'd changed and that I wasn't like that before. He was right: I wasn't 'me'. Now I am, and I'm starting to accept myself for who I am. I no longer contain myself all the time and I don't use that smile that made my face ache every night. I'm

---

[89] Non-literal expression used to indicate something that implies significant effort.

enjoying being me, but it's a painful process, too." (Carolina, 36 years old).

Many of the autistic women that I've diagnosed mention that now they can remove this mask in their safe spaces, with their partners, families and friends, they've felt a sense of rejection, or at least perplexity by these people, who are 'annoyed' by this change. This is the consequence of masking: you've created such a perfect representation of reality that you've managed to trick even those who are closest to you. The more intense the masking, the more perplexed reactions you'll receive from those around you. For me, this is the warning sign that you've gone too far and need to deconstruct this mask for the emotional and cognitive wellbeing of the autistic person.

Either way, your home environment should be safe and mask-free. This is where an autistic people should feel completely free to be themselves: stimming, any movements that help them to regulate, routines, recurrent topics, time alone… everything. You need to let your autistic self go. You have to do it, because out there in a social context, you might find it more beneficial to restrict yourself.

SIGNS OF CONTINOUS MASKING

PRE-DIAGNOSIS	POST-DIAGNOSIS
- MEMORY LOSS	PROPORTIONAL SOCIAL DISTANCING
- SUBSTANCE USE (ALCOHOL, DRUGS)	
- DEREALISATION	(THE CLOSER THE INTIMACY CIRCLE, THE MORE INTENSE THE MASKING)
- DEPERSONALISATION	

Be wary of these signs.

This is, of course, a personal decision. When I work with people who have been masking and are now starting to be themselves, I warn them that not everyone will accept their true (and new, for them) self. That's why I think that starting in your safe place, at home, and gradually expanding to your relationship circles (as we saw in chapter 7) is a good move. Or, in other words, this generally means that the closer to the family circle, the less masking we should be doing.

"As soon as I stopped masking, I lost lots of the people I considered to be my friends. Although it was tough, it has now given me a sense of freedom" (Sara, 31 years old).

In those contexts and situations where they don't want to or don't feel safe and free to be themselves, people on the spectrum tend to develop a series of compensation strategies. Lists, scripts and diagrams for decision-making that many autistic people create as a 'guide' to follow during different social situations have clear limitations. Firstly, interactions are far too quick to remember what they can and can't do or say, which makes the autistic person appear slow and mechanical in their interaction. And secondly, and most importantly, social contexts are incredibly variable and there's no decision-making tree, nor one that covers all possibilities. In any case, contexts with a strict protocol or specific behaviour rules or labels which limit the number of spontaneous situations. But even in these contexts, anything can happen.

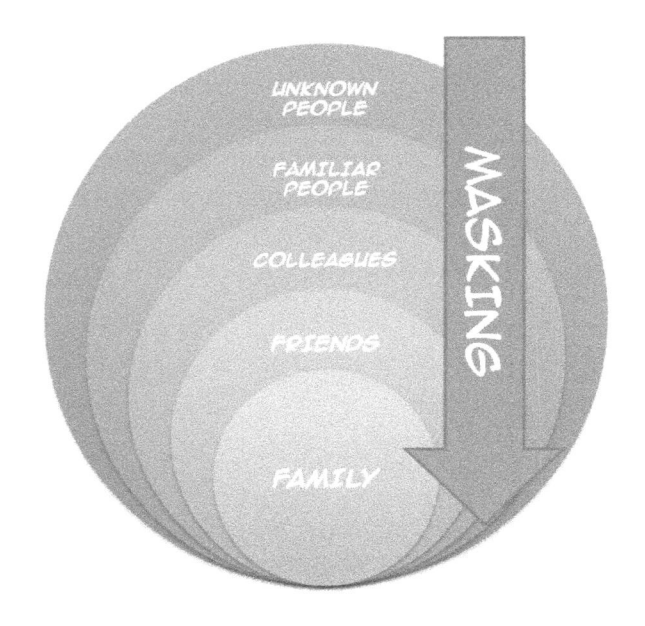

Tell me where you mask and I'll tell you the consequences.

"I've been a transatlantic pilot for many years. In fact, I'm one of Spain's most honoured commercial pilots. I've been in thousands of situations, landings and even emergency landings. But I've never had such a bad time as when I'd go out for dinner with my colleagues. I didn't know how to act, and even they appeared to be different people. While on the plane, I work with protocols. In life, I need protocols (Juan Antonio, 55 years old).

Masking should be replaced, in any case, by specific tools to avoid the potential impact of its continued use. In an ideal scenario, no autistic person would have to mask at any point in their life. But we know that this world, being incredibly cruel and unfair, won't openly welcome a type of behaviour that isn't deemed acceptable by the majority. Therefore, while we highlight the importance of opening our minds as regards the different forms of neurodivergence, we should consciously put up on our autistic armour, so as not to be gobbled up by the world around us.

Epilogue

Sculpting your autistic armour

"I went through a type of mourning because of the word autism and the myths surrounding it. That initial mourning then became a sense of freedom" (Lorena, 29 years old).

A while ago, I was working with an autistic person who was training in the computing sector, more specifically in software testing[90], and they said this:

- Daniel, why do I have to wear a shirt to work?
- Because there's a protocol. You could go wearing a polo shirt or a certain type of trainers, but you need to keep in mind that your clothes need to match and need to give the right impression.
- But that's not me. If I dress like that, I'm deceiving people, which for me is like lying.
- You're right, in some ways it is.
- So, why do I have to do it?
- Dressing a certain way is linked to respect for what you do and shows your concern for the impression you might give. It's not so much about the type of clothes, but more about them being well

---

[90] Software testing refers to undertaking tests on a computer product in order to evaluate its quality and any potential errors.

> *looked after, clean and ironed. If this isn't the case, they might think that you don't take your work seriously and you might be judged for your appearance instead of your performance. Think of your work clothes as your armour protecting you from prejudice.*
- *I like that!*

Throughout this book I've tried to create a vision of autism as a developmental condition, a type of neurodivergence that manifests as a unique and extraordinary dimension, and at the same time, as a myriad of manifestations, but with a series of processes that occur in each and every person on the spectrum, from children to adults. An awareness of this unique way of processing and perceiving the world is fundamental, both for the autistic person and for the people in their lives. More ambitiously, for the world in general.

"I would explain my daughter's diagnosis to her as soon as possible. It's self-awareness and an understanding of why she experiences certain things. This will allow her to find out how she can regulate herself and to understand that she needs to stop and rest at certain times during the day. It means telling her she's autistic, she's different and that's ok, and she has every right to be herself. And, on the other hand, we need to teach society to get rid of the stigma that makes autism seem like a terminal cancer diagnosis" (Carolina, 36 years old).

Autistic people are constantly having to fight, eternally trying to fit into this world, trying to adapt to the expectations of neurotypical people, which means that the majority (to a more or lesser extent) face significant challenges in terms of feeling like secure, valued and competent individuals.

Realistically, we know that while educating society, autistic people should protect themselves and develop certain strategies to avoid succumbing to the pressures of an incredibly stressful and arbitrary world that only really works for the majority of neurotypical people. I always tend to tell the autistic people I work with that their way of being, perceiving and processing isn't anything bad, but at certain times, in certain environments and with certain people, this way of being can lead the other person to make an inaccurate judgment about them and it may lead to certain consequences. This is, of course, unfair, but it's reality and sadly, a common occurrence.

Generally speaking, and summarising everything we've seen throughout this book, these are the key points and most important tasks:

1) Embrace your autistic condition: for an autistic person, embracing their condition and everything it represents is important. You need to discover your way of processing information because human beings tend to contemplate others when it comes to situating challenges and skills. For an autistic person, this is incredibly unfair, because if they compare themselves to a neurotypical person and what they can or cannot do, is going to be a very unfair comparison. Many autistic people 'force' themselves to be like other people on the spectrum, which is a losing battle. It's as if a bird were to compare its skills with those of a mammal. The autistic person should establish more plausible references such as other people on the spectrum who have a similar 'operating system'. There are no limits in terms of what an autistic person can achieve, but they'll only be able to achieve things if they use their skills, abilities and strengths correctly.

2) Your home should be your refuge: the outside world is stressful enough without us being unable to be our true

selves at home. And of course, everyone who lives with someone on the spectrum should be aware not only of their diagnosis, but also the nature of the condition itself. You should be able to feel free to be yourself at home, with everything that entails: never stop yourself from stimming, spending time enjoying your interests, being alone or be incredibly literal without having to explain to people that there are no hidden intentions behind your directness during conversation.

Daniel Millán López
@dmillanlopez

Personas #autistas del mundo. Vuestra casa es vuestra fortaleza. Es el lugar donde poder desplegar a vuestras anchas vuestras conductas, rutinas, intereses... Suficiente os obliga a reprimiros la sociedad como para que vuestra propia casa no podáis ser vosotres mismes.
#TEA #CEA

Tweet[91] by @dmillanlopez. Superman's Fortress of Solitude: a brilliant autistic analogy.

---

[91] Autistic people around the world. Your home is your fortress. It's where you can engage in your behaviours, routines, interests... the fact society forces you to suppress your true self is enough, let alone not being able to be yourself in your own home. #TEA #CEA #ASD #ASC

3) Regulate your energy levels: when you have to leave your refuge, plan your activities, meetings and tasks well, establishing a start, finish and your goals. Remember that the outside world can be incredibly stressful, a source of sensory overwhelm and very unpredictable. According to Nick Dubin (2009): "neurotypical people learn and assimilate the concept of unpredictability and just accept it as part of their life. For some reason, we don't". Remember: shit happens. But what you can do is to jot down the overwhelming situations and make an estimation as to how much energy you'll have left, to make the appropriate adjustments. Pack anything that could help with sensory regulation, such as sunglasses, noise cancelling headphones or stim toys or objects. If you need to use tools in order to be able to face the neurotypical world, do just that. Make sure you plan in certain rest times throughout the day and from one day to the next.

4) The autistic community: find other people on the spectrum to start relationships with. In accordance with Locke (2010), autistic people go in search of each other and are more comfortable in each other's company. If I'm honest, I'm surprised people have ever thought anything else. We all create networks based on aspects we share with other people, whether they be likes/dislikes, hobbies, sharing a task or project. In autism, it's totally normal to gravitate naturally towards other people who may think and feel similarly when you discover your way of thinking, processing and feeling is different. In my experience, I've found that lots of autistic people have ended up in a relationship with someone for their similarities, and then later discovered

that they're both on the spectrum. It's not a coincidence.

5) Find support from professionals in the field of autism who are not ableist and who have an up-to-date, realistic perspective of autism. A neurotypical person who is able to genuinely empathise and understand how an autistic person processes and perceives reality can offer you a series of tools and techniques that can help you manage in the neurotypical world.

This autistic guide was created with the aim of offering autistic people tips on how to face this unpredictable, unfair and stressful world through an understanding of their condition. There are few things in this world that frustrate me more than seeing someone with huge potential doomed to never achieve their goals due to a lack of understanding of themselves and an unawareness of how their surroundings impact their abilities. If just one autistic person finds something in this book that helps them improve their self-awareness and better themselves in any one area of their life, the work put into writing it will have been totally worth it.

Questionnaires

The following questionnaires may give you a rough indication if you suspect you or your child may be on the autistic spectrum. Remember that these are just rough indications and are by no means a clinical diagnosis. Consider the results carefully and consult professionals in order to verify your suspicions. The questionnaires are available as a PDF download on my website: www.danielmillanlopez.com.

The first is CHAT, a questionnaire developed by Baron-Cohen in 1992 in order to detect autism in children aged 18 months, or if they're slightly older, at school age. I made some adaptations for the Spanish reader.

The second questionnaire is the Childhood Asperger Syndrome Test (CAST) created by Fiona J. Scott, together with Simon Baron-Cohen, Patrick Bolton and Carol Byrne. As in the previous questionnaire, I've slightly amended it based on my experience over the years.

The third questionnaire is the Adult Asperger Assessment (AAA) which was also created by Baron-Cohen, together with other researchers. Here, I also made some adaptations following years of experience using this assessment on autistic adults.

Lastly, you'll find a questionnaire that I've translated to detect autistic masking behaviours, the CAT-Q (Laura Hull, Baron-Cohen, among others).

Questionnaire 1 – Suspicions of autism, ASD/ASC

CHAT- Autism risk questionnaire by Baren-Cohen et al., 1992

This is a questionnaire for parents to fill out. Fill out one of these two questionnaires if you suspect autism or autism spectrum disorder (ASD/ASC).

Questionnaire 1. 1. Age around 18 months.

Answer Yes or No to the following questions and add up the number of "No" answers. You can find a results table at the end of the questionnaire.

1.	Does your child enjoy and get involved in games such as *This little piggy*, *peek-a-boo*, jumping on your knees, etc?	Yes	No
2.	Do they show interest in their peers?	Yes	No
3.	Does your child simulate with objects, playing 'as if' things were something other than what they are? (For example, acting as if a construction block or box was a car).	Yes[1]	No
4.	Does your child ever point with their	Yes	No

	finger to ask for something or bring something to your attention?		
5.	Does your child know how to play adequately with small toys or miniatures (for example, cars or blocks) as opposed to just putting them to their mouth, touching them, throwing them or hitting them).	Yes	No
6.	Get your child's attention and show them an interesting object across the room and say "Oh, look! There's a *toy name*". Observe your child's face. Do they look towards what you're showing them?	Yes[2]	No
7.	Get your child's attention and give them a car, a glass, a spoon, a plate and a doll. Observe whether or not they simulate doing something with these objects (for example, as if the doll was getting into the car, feeding them, etc).	Yes[3]	No
8.	Ask your child, "Where's the light?". Do they point to the light with their index finger?	Yes[4]	No

Results:

0- NOT AUTISM or ASD/ASC.
1 or 2 – MODERATE RISK. We recommend monitoring.
3 or + - HIGH RISK. Contact a professional.

Notes
(1) Before responding Yes, ensure that there's a sign that the child really believes that the object is the car (for example, accompanied by noises).
(2) Before responding Yes, ensure that they haven't just looked at your hand, but have actually looked at the object you're point at.
(3) If they can elicit any other example of simulating with any other object, answer Yes.
(4) Repeat this with "Where's the bear?" or with any other unreachable object, if they don't understand the word "light". Before responding Yes to this question, they should have looked at your face when pointing.

Questionnaire 1.2. School Age

Circle the answer that best describes your child's behaviour. The results can be found at the end of the questionnaire.

F: Frequently | O: Often | OC: Occasionally | N: Never

1.	They don't respond to their name being called.	F	O	OC	N
2.	They don't point to show something that's happening or that they can see.	F	O	OC	N
3.	They don't speak or has stopped speaking.	F	O	OC	N
4.	Their language is repetitive and barely functional.	F	O	OC	N

286

5.	They use people as if they were tools to get what they want.	F	O	OC	N
6.	They generally communicate to ask for something or say no, not to make comments.	F	O	OC	N
7.	They don't react to what is happening around them.	F	O	OC	N
8.	They don't show interest in the relationship with others, don't try and get their attention and sometimes rejects them.	F	O	OC	N
9.	They don't look at faces or make eye contact while smiling.	F	O	OC	N
10.	They don't engage with other children, nor imitate them.	F	O	OC	N
11.	They don't look towards where you're pointing.	F	O	OC	N
12.	They use toys in a peculiar way (spinning, lining up, throwing…)	F	O	OC	N
13.	Lack of social, symbolic or imaginative play ("Acting as though…")	F	O	OC	N
14.	Their games are repetitive.	F	O	OC	N
15.	Lines up or orders things unnecessarily.	F	O	OC	N
16.	They are very sensitive to certain textures, sounds, smells or tastes.	F	O	OC	N

17. They do strange, repetitive movements.	F	O	OC	N
18. They throw tantrums or resist environmental changes.	F	O	OC	N
19. They have an unusual attachment to some objects of specific visual stimuli.	F	O	OC	N
20. They laugh or cry without an obvious cause.	F	O	OC	N
21. They have good visual-spatial abilities.	F	O	OC	N

Results:

If you have answered F or O for more than 5 statements, we recommend you contact professionals in order to undergo a diagnostic assessment.

Questionnaire 2 – Suspicions of Asperger's Syndrome – ASD/ASC Level 1

Test for Asperger's Syndrome in childhood (CAST), by Fiona J. Scott, Simon Baron-Cohen, Patrick Bolton and Carol Brayne.

Complete the questionnaire if you suspect Asperger's Syndrome or ASD/ASC Level 1. Questionnaire for children.

1. Do they tend to play with their peers, with no obvious difficulties?	Yes	No
2. Do they tend to come over spontaneously to talk to you?	Yes	No

3. Did they speak at 2 years old?   Yes   No

4. Do they like sports?   Yes   No

5. Do you think fitting into a group (friends, family...) is important to them?   Yes   No

6. Do they tend to focus on unusual details other people don't tend to notice?   Yes   No

7. Do they tend to take everything literally?   Yes   No

8. At 3 years old, did they spend a lot of time "acting"? (For example: as if they were a superhero, or in a play kitchen).   Yes   No

9. Do they tend to do things in the same way, repeatedly?   Yes   No

10. Do they find interacting with their peers easy?   Yes   No

11. Can they follow two conversations at the same time?   Yes   No

12. Are they at the appropriate reading age?	Yes	No
13. Do they have the same interests as other children their age?	Yes	No
14. Do they have any particular interests they spend a lot of time on?	Yes	No
15. Do they have "real friends"? (Other than "classmates", "neighbours" or "acquaintances".	Yes	No
16. Do they often bring you things they're interested in showing you?	Yes	No
17. Do they tend to have fun making jokes or playing pranks?	Yes	No
18. Do they struggle to understand any social norms?	Yes	No
19. Do they appear to have an unusual memory when it comes to details?	Yes	No
20. Is their voice 'unusual'? (For example: almost like an adult, flat, monotone, without a rhythm or high-pitched).	Yes	No

21. Are other people important to them?	Yes	No
22. Can they get dressed and undressed independently?	Yes	No
23. Are they good at conversing? (Letting others speak and waiting their turn)	Yes	No
24. Do they play imaginatively with other children, 'acting things out'?	Yes	No
25. To they tend to say things without thinking?	Yes	No
26. Can they count to 50 without missing out any numbers?	Yes	No
27. Do they maintain 'normal' eye contact?	Yes	No
28. Do they engage in unusual or repetitive body movements?	Yes	No
29. Would you say their social behaviour is 'inflexible'?	Yes	No
30. Do they tend to say "you" or "he" when they really want to say "I"?	Yes	No

31. Do they prefer to engage in imaginative activities, such as acting or telling stories over creating or reading lists of facts or numbers?   Yes   No

32. Does the person they're talking to sometimes get fed up of them because they don't explain what they're talking about? (They don't set the scene before telling the story).   Yes   No

33. Can they ride a bike? (Without stabilisers)   Yes   No

34. Do they try and create routines for themselves or others in a way that causes issues?   Yes   No

35. Are they worried about what others think of them?   Yes   No

36. Do they tend to end up talking about their favourite topic instead of following the conversation started by the other person?   Yes   No

37. Do they tend to use unusual or strange words or phrases?   Yes   No

Scoring

Add a point if your answer coincides with the following:

0-	No	23-	No
1-	No	24-	No
2-	No point (control question)	25-	Yes
3-	No point (control question)	26-	No point (control question)
4-	No	27-	No
5-	Yes	28-	Yes
6-	Yes	29-	Yes
7-	No	30-	Yes
8-	Yes	31-	No
9-	No	32-	Yes
10-	No	33-	No point (control question)
11-	No point (control question)	34-	Yes
12-	No	35-	No
13-	Yes	36-	Yes
14-	No	37-	Yes
15-	No		
16-	No		
17-	Yes		
18-	Yes		
19-	Yes		

20- No point (control question)
21- No point (control question)

Results:

Questions 3, 4, 12, 21, 22, 26 and 33 don't score any points. Add up all the points and if the total is equal to or more than 15, we recommend you contact a professional in order to undergo a diagnostic assessment. If the total is less than 5, there's no initial indication of Asperger's Syndrome – ASD/ASC Level 1. If the total is between 6 and 14 points, contact a professional in order to undergo additional screening tests.

Questionnaire 3 – Suspicions of Asperger's Syndrome – ASD/ASC 1

Adult Asperger Assessment (AAA), by Baron-Cohen, S.; Wheelwright, S.; Robinson, J.; Woodbury-Smith, M.R.

Fill in this questionnaire if you suspect Asperger's Syndrome – ASD/ASC Level 1. Questionnaire for ages 16 and older.

A. Areas related to social interaction

Notable deficit in the use of multiple non-verbal behaviours such as eye contact, facial expression, corporeal posture and gestures that regulate social interaction.	Yes	No
2. Evident difficulties when trying to establish relationships with their peers (for example: work or classmates).	Yes	No
3. Doesn't show much interest in pleasing others. Does not tend to share personal experiences (or when they do, they lack detail). They don't look for people with whom	Yes	No

to share their interests.

4. Difficulties when it comes to responding to the emotional demands of others.	Yes	No
5. Difficulty understanding complex social situations.	Yes	No
6. Difficulty understanding the thoughts and feelings of other people.	Yes	No

B. Areas related to behaviour

1. They show one or more stereotyped and restricted interest of abnormal intensity or focus.	Yes	No
2. They undertake non-functional rituals. They establish minimally flexible routines, with no obvious function.	Yes	No
3. They engage in repetitive movements, especially in situations of stress and anxiety (rocking or hand flapping, for example).	Yes	No
4. They tend to think in terms of all or nothing (for example, regarding politics or morals) instead of being open to other perspectives.	Yes	No

C. Areas related to communication

1.	Tends to bring any conversation back to themselves or their interests.	Yes	No
2.	Notable difficulties starting or maintaining a conversation.	Yes	No
3.	They do not understand superficial social contact with others, spending time with other people without arguments, debates or activities. They don't understand subtleties.	Yes	No
4.	Lack of ability to recognise boredom or lack of interest in their listener. They know they shouldn't talk too much about their interests, but this difficulty occurs if this topic is raised.	Yes	No
5.	They often tend to say things without thinking about the emotional impact this may have on the other person.	Yes	No

D. Areas related to imagination

1.	Symbolic play without variety or spontaneity according to their developmental age.	Yes	No
2.	Lack of ability to spontaneously tell, read or create a fictional story, without copying.	Yes	No
3.	Their interest in fiction (book or drama) is limited to possible real facts (for example, science fiction, history, technical film aspects).	Yes	No

E. Prior requirements

1.	Delay or abnormal functioning in each of the previous sections (A-D) throughout their development.	Yes	No
2.	The disorder causes clinically significant deficits in social, work and other important functional areas.	Yes	No
3.	They have not shown clinically significant delay in cognitive development, acquisition of skills in accordance with their age group that allow them to be independent, adaptive behaviour (not related to social interaction or skills related to social interaction, for example, personal hygiene).	Yes	No

Results:

The result is deemed positive and a diagnostic assessment undertaken by a professional is recommended if 3 or more "yes" answers are marked in sections A and C; 2 or more in section B; and at least one in section D. All 3 answers in section E should be marked "yes".

Autistic camouflaging questionnaire

The Camouflaging Autistic Traits Questionnaire (CAT-Q), by Laura Hull, William Mandy, Meng Chuan Lai, Simon Baron-Cohen, Carrie Allison, Paula Smith and K. V. Petrides.

Complete this questionnaire if you suspect you might be masking. Rate the following statements according to how much you agree with them in terms of your current situation, with 1 being "Strongly disagree" and 7 being "Strongly agree".

SECTION ONE

When I'm interacting with someone, I deliberately copy their body language or facial expressions.	1	2	3	4	5	6	7
I learn how people use their bodies and faces to interact with others by watching TV, films or reading books.	1	2	3	4	5	6	7
I've tried to improve my understanding of social skills by observing others.	1	2	3	4	5	6	7
I repeat phrases exactly as I heard them the first time.	1	2	3	4	5	6	7
I practice my facial expressions and body language and try to use them when interacting with others.	1	2	3	4	5	6	7

I spend time learning social skills by watching TV or films and try to use what I've learned, in my own interactions.	1	2	3	4	5	6	7
In social interactions, I use behaviours I've learned by observing others.	1	2	3	4	5	6	7
I've discovered the rules of social interaction (for example studying psychology or reading books on human behaviour), which has improved my own social skills.	1	2	3	4	5	6	7
I've created different protocols to use in different social skills (for example, lists of questions or conversation topics).	1	2	3	4	5	6	7

SECTION TWO

I examine my own body language and facial expressions to make them seem natural.	1	2	3	4	5	6	7
I adapt my body language and facial expressions to appear relaxed.	1	2	3	4	5	6	7
I monitor my body language and facial expressions to try and	1	2	3	4	5	6	7

make myself appear interested in the person I'm interacting with.							
I adapt my body language and facial expressions to try and make myself appear interested in the person I'm interacting with.	1	2	3	4	5	6	7
I don't feel the need to make eye contact with other people if I don't want to.	1	2	3	4	5	6	7
During social interaction, I don't pay attention to my facial expressions nor corporeal posture.	1	2	3	4	5	6	7
I always think about the impression I make on other people.	1	2	3	4	5	6	7
I'm always aware of the impression I make on other people.	1	2	3	4	5	6	7

SECTION THREE

I feel the need to play a role in order to be successful in a specific social situation.	1	2	3	4	5	6	7
When I talk to other people, I feel as though the conversa-	1	2	3	4	5	6	7

tion flows naturally.							
I try and avoid interacting with others in social situations.	1	2	3	4	5	6	7
I feel as though I'm playing a role, more than being myself, when I interact with others in social situations.	1	2	3	4	5	6	7
I have to force myself to interact with others in social situations.	1	2	3	4	5	6	7
I feel as though I'm 'trying to be normal' when I interact with others.	1	2	3	4	5	6	7
I need support from someone in order to socialise.	1	2	3	4	5	6	7
I don't feel free to be myself when I'm around other people.	1	2	3	4	5	6	7

Results

Add up the total points for each of the three sections.
The maximum for the first section is 63.
The maximum for the second section is 56.
The maximum for the third section is 56.

In order to consider clinical symptoms of camouflaging, the total score for the second and third sections individually should be greater than the first section.

2nd section > 1st section
3rd section > 1st section

Total scores over 31 in the first section and 28 in the second and third sections are reason for concern, and I recommend you contact a professional.

Acknowledgements

I wouldn't have been able to write this book without the input and unconditional support of the love of my life, Laura Alberola, and Carmen López, my mother – an avid reader unlike anyone I've ever known – who persisted in begging me to get some of my knowledge of autism on paper, even if it was just something short. My brother Pepucho, Belén and my nephews, Miguel and Luís. Marisa, for her artwork and for giving me that final burst of motivation. Jai, for the incredible English translation you're reading. Andrea, for proofreading and giving me advice. This book would never have come to light with without the insistence of the autistic community and their families who begged me to write it. My friend Marina and my dear neurodivergent *sisters,* Neurodivergente and Aida, and Carmen and all the women at CEPAMA. My team of traitors, Eva and Javi. My ConoCEA group on Telegram and the wonderful autistic community and their families on Twitter, YouTube and Instagram. The professionals who work within the field of autism and neurodivergence with respect and without being condescending. To all the autistic adults and their families who have put their trust in me. And, in particular, all the autistic children I've worked with, am working with and will work with, for keeping me humble.

Sketches

As I'm always in search of coherence, I knew I wanted an autistic person to illustrate this book. As you've seen throughout this book, visuals are a fundamental part of life for all autistic people. Many of the illustrations in this book reflect their experiences, so who better to bring these experiences to life than someone on the spectrum?

Marisa's work is nothing short of spectacular, even more so considering that sometimes my sketches of my own ideas were somewhat basic. Sometimes she needed additional instructions to be able to understand what I was after, as you can see below in this illustration for chapter 11.

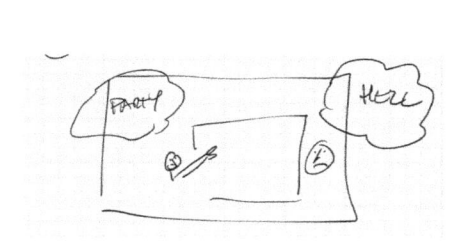

My sketch.   **Marisa's sketch.**

On other occasions however, (and in Marisa's words), my more detailed ideas made things much easier (page 204).

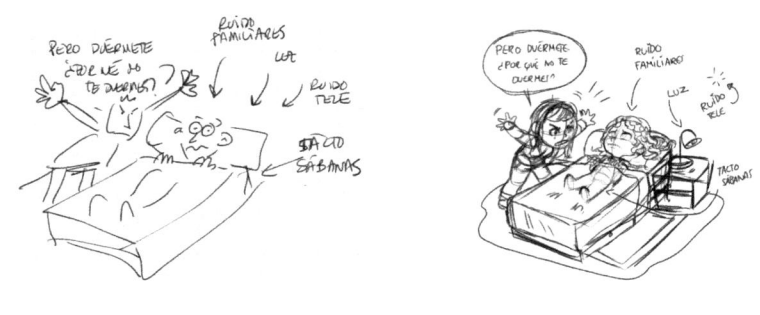

My sketch.   **Marisa's sketch**

During the first stages of creating the style for the book, Marisa would send me different options until we found the best style or expressions for each of the illustrated situations. Here are some snippets of the search for the final drawings on pages 102 and 115 respectively.

We chose C5 and A2

In search of the most convincing angry expression.

Autistic people identify so much with the different situations we included, that Marisa herself wanted to be included in one of them. This is her sketch of the illustration on page 74.

As you'll have noticed, I'm in many of the illustrated situations we described, as I've experienced them first-hand with autistic people. The search for my avatar was one of Marisa's first tasks, and we really did have a laugh.

Goal: to not look *too* much like Pablo Iglesias[92].

Of course, the cover took a while for obvious reasons. I wanted to include an illustration that reflected many of the difficulties and obstacles faced by people on the spectrum. At the time, Marisa mentioned we could do something similar to a "Battle Royale", which was really popular at the time. After creating the illustrations, I sent Marisa a sketch of a few autistic

---

[92] Pablo Iglesias is a Spanish politician known for his long hair tied back in a ponytail.

people, armed and defending themselves from some metaphorical monsters who represent historic and current threats against them.

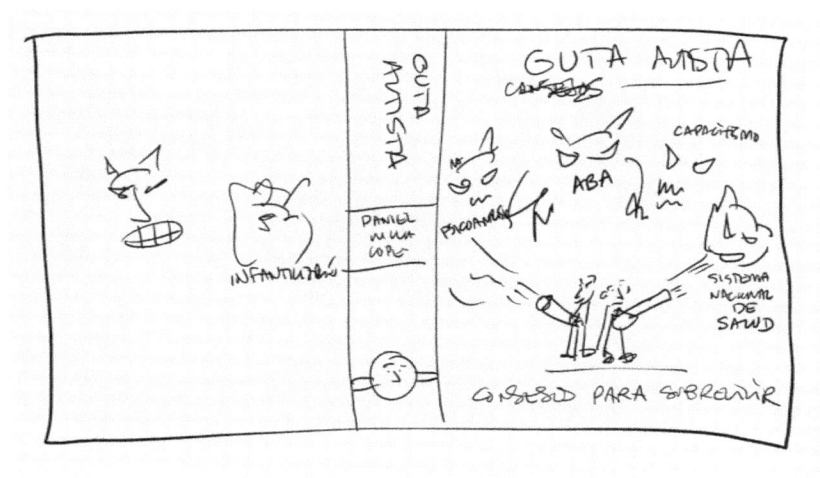

My sad looking sketch.

Marisa's draft.

Outlines of the characters.

Colour test.

And the final design.

Bibliography

Abelenda, A.J; Rodríguez E. (2020): Evidencia científica en integración sensorial como abordaje de terapia ocupacional en autismo. Medicina. Buenos Aires. Vol. 80 (Sup. II): 41-46

Albores, L., Hernández, L., Díaz, J. A. & Cortés, B. (2008): Dificultades en la evaluación y diagnóstico del autismo. Una discusión. Salud Mental, 31, 37- 44

Ayres, J. (1998): La integración sensorial y el niño. Trillas. Méjico.

Barker, C. & Galasinski, D. (2001): Cultural studies and discourse analysis: A dialogue on language and identity. Sage. Londres.

Barkley, R., A. (1998): Attention Deficit Hyperactivity Disorder: A Handbook for Diagnosis and Treatment. The Journal of Clinical Psychiatry.

Baron-Cohen et al. (2013): Do girls with anorexia nervosa have elevated autistic traits? -Mol Autism. 2013 Jul 31;4(1):24. doi: 10.1186/2040-2392-4-24.

Baron-Cohen, S., Johnson, D., Asher, J., Wheelwright, S., Fisher, SE, Gregersen, PK, et al. (2013): ¿La sinestesia es más común en el autismo? Molecular Autism. 4:40. doi: 10.1186 / 2040-2392-4-40

Baron-Cohen, S., Leslie, A. M. & Frith U (1985): Does the autistic child have a theory of mind? Cognition, 21, 37 – 46.

Beck, A., Rush, A., Shaw, B. & Emery, G. (1979): Terapia cognitiva de la depresión. Desclee de Bouwer. Madrid.

Bengoechea, M. (2019): Razones de la lingüística feminista para abogar por un lenguaje inclusivo. Centro de Estudios Políticos y Constitucionales en colaboración con Clásicas y Modernas. Madrid.

Bogdashina O. (2007): Percepción Sensorial en Autismo y Asperger. Autismo Ávila. Ávila.

Courchesne E, Mouton PR, Calhoun ME, Semendeferi K, Ahrens-Barbeau C, Hallet MJ, Barnes CC, Pierce K. (2011): Neuron number and size in prefrontal cortex of children with autism. JAMA. 306(18):2001-2010.

Dovern A. et al. J. Neurosci. 32, 7614-7621 (2012) PubMed.

Dubin, N (2009): Asperger Syndrome and anxiety. A guide to successful stress management. Jessica Kingsley Publishers. Londres.

Elbe D, & Lalani Z (2012): Review of the pharmacotherapy of irritability of autism. Journal of the Canadian Academy of Child and Adolescent Psychiatry = Journal de l'Academie canadienne de psychiatrie de l'enfant et de l'adolescent, 21 (2), 130-46 PMID: 22548111.

George, R. y Stokes, M. A. (2018): Sexual orientation in autism spectrum disorder. Autism Research, 11(1), 133-141.

Green RM, Travers AM, Howe Y, McDougle CJ. Women and Autism Spectrum Disorder (2019): Diagnosis and Implications for Treatment of Adolescents and Adults. Curr Psychiatry Rep. 2019; 21:22.

Guido Lagos Garay (2004): Gregory Bateson: un pensamiento (complejo) para pensar la complejidad. Un intento de lectura/escritura terapéutica. Revista Latinoamericana. Polis.

Hinshaw, S., Peele, P., y Danielson, L. (2001): Public salud issues in ADHD: individual, system, and cost burden of the disorder workshop. Centers for Disease Control and Prevention. Estados Unidos.

Hull L, Mandy W, Lai M-C, et al. (2018): Development and Validation of the Camouflaging Autistic Traits Questionnaire (CAT-Q). J. doi:10.1007/s10803-018-3792-6

Kumazaki H, Muramatsu T, Miyao M, Okada KI, Mimura M, Kikuchi M (2019): Brief Report: Olfactory Adaptation in Children with Autism Spectrum Disorders. J Autism Dev Disord. doi: 10.1007/s10803-019-04053-6.

Lee MK, Guilleminault C. (2002): Rapid Eye Movement Sleep-related Parasomnias. Curr Treat Options. Neurol 2002; 4: 113-120.

Margolis KG, Li Z, Stevanovic K, Saurman V, Israelyan N, Anderson GM, Snyder I, Veenstra-VanderWeele J, Blakely RD, Gershon MD (2016): Serotonin transporter variant drives preventable gastrointestinal abnormalities in development and function. J Clin Invest Apr 25. pii: 84877.

Margolis, K.G., Buie, T.M., Turner, J.B. et al. (2019): Development of a Brief Parent-Report Screen for Common Gastrointestinal.Disorders in Autism Spectrum Disorder. J Autism Dev Dis-ord 49, 349–362.

Martos, J; Llorente, M; González; Ayuda, R; Freire, S. (2013). Los niños pequeños con autismo: soluciones prácticas para problemas cotidianos. Equipo Deletrea. Madrid.

Mesibov G. y Howlesy M. (2010): El acceso al currículo por alum-nos con trastornos del espectro del autismo: uso del programa Teacch para favorecer la inclusión. Autismo Ávila. Ávila.

Myles, B.S., Cook, K.T., Miller, N.E., Rinner, L., & Robbins, L. (2000): Asperger Syndrome and sensory issues: Practical solutions for making sense of the world. Shawnee Mission. KS: Autism Asperger Publishing Company.

Onandia, I. y Millán D. (2020): Mitos en Autismo y TDAH con Iban Onandia. YouTube: https://youtu.be/U3ANnARLVbc.

Onandia, I., Sánchez M., Oltra, Javier (2019): Evaluación neuropsicológica de los procesos atencionales. Síntesis. Madrid.

Pin-Arboledas, G. (2019): El sueño del niño con trastornos del neuro-desarrollo. Medicina. 79. 44-50.

Pedinielli, J. (1992): Psychosomatique et alexithymie. PUF. Paris.

Peeters, Theo (1994): Autism. From Theoretical Understanding to Educational Intervention. Wiley-Blackwell. New Jersey.

Peeters, Theo (2008): Autismo: De la comprensión teórica a la intervención educativa. Autismo Ávila. Ávila.

Riviere, A. y Martos, J. (1998): El tratamiento del Autismo. Nuevas perspectivas. Madrid. Ministerio de Trabajo y Asuntos Sociales.

Simone, R. (2010): Aspergirls: Empowering Females with Asperger's Syndrome. Jessica Kingsley Publishers. Londres.

Stokes, T. F. & Baer, D. M. (1977): An implicit technology of generalization. Journal of Applied Behavior Analysis, 10, 349-367.

Sukhareva E. (2015): Prior to Asperger and Kanner. Nordic Journal of Psychiatry.

Tavassoli T, Baron-Cohen S. (2012): Olfactory detection thresholds and adaptation in adults with autism spectrum condition. J Autism De-velop Dis 42(6): 905–909.

Toth, K., Dawson, G., Meltzoff, A. N., Greenson, J. & Fein, D. (2007): Early social, Imitation play, and language abilities of young non-autistic siblings of children with autism. Journal of Autism and Developmental Disorders, 37, 145-157.

Urtega, G; Fernández R; Durán, P. (2016): Intervención en el en-torno escolar desde terapia ocupacional. Colegio de terapeutas ocupacionales de Navarra. Navarra.

Van Steensel, F.J.A., Bogels, S.M., & Perrin, S.(2011): Anxiety disorders in children and adolescents with autistic spectrum disorders: A metaanalysis. Clinical Child and Family Psychology Review, 14, 302-317.